# Gus

## One Woman's Champion

### Victoria Yablonsky

GUS: ONE WOMAN'S CHAMPION. Copyright © 2021 by Victoria Yablonsky. All rights reserved. Printed in the United States of America. No part of this book may be used or reproduced in any manner whatsoever without written permission except in the case of brief quotations embodied in critical articles and reviews. For information, address Outrun Press, 212 Long Hill Road, Hillsborough, NJ 08844.

ISBN: 978-0-9834845-5-4

Library of Congress Control Number: 2020950493

# *Acknowledgments*

I could not let this book out into the world without acknowledging the many contributions from generous readers along the way. Many of you have had a lasting impact on this narrative.

I wish to thank Outrun Press for their interest in this project.

I wish to thank Michael McLeod for valuable advice about style and readability; I did not always take his advice, but I always appreciated it. I thank Perry Hodges and Herb Marks for their careful reading of a late draft. The suggestions they made and the fascinating discussion it engendered made me see what a truly literary sensibility might have made of this material, rather than a humble memoirist like myself.

I reserve greatest thanks for three wonderful readers: Sara Jameson, Louise Yelin, and Lori Chamberlain; Sara for helping me early on to sketch in the parameters, the texture, the essential point of the story, Louise for helping me organize necessary material more efficiently and making the whole more readable, and Lori for a rigorous reading of the whole for tone and logic. You have each made it better than it would have otherwise been, and I hope each of you will see your handiwork in the final product.

For permission to quote, I would like to thank Tony McCallum and Jessica Saukkonen for their eloquent passages taken from Facebook threads. I would like to thank *The Gather* for both cover picture credits. I would like to thank Scrogo for the front and back cover design.

I would like to thank Mark and Adrienne Deller for their immense hospitality and for trusting me with their flocks and fields. I am deeply indebted to them. I am, and will be forever, the richer for it.

I would like to thank the many, many top handlers, stockmen, breeders, and sheepdog enthusiasts both in the US and the UK for their notable comments on sheepdog training and sheepdogs, and the array of top handlers who gave me lessons that immeasurably changed my understanding of how to handle and train a border collie. In particular, I would like to thank Haley Hunewill for sharing her vast knowledge of sheep and dogs.

I owe a huge debt of gratitude to my husband, Robert Edelman, for his excitement about, and encouragement of, my project, for taking time away from his own writing to read mine, and for assimilating my discussions about training and trialing to narratives about sport in general. It added a dimension and an authority to the whole. His encouragement and support have made all the difference.

And, finally, I wish to thank Libby Nieder for her invaluable advice so many years ago that I buy Gus as a yearling and for her unfailing admiration for him his life long. With her greater understanding, she was truer to him than I was myself. And even though I thought Gus's naughty spots were so outlandish that I almost sent him back the week I got him, from that moment on, we became a team.

# *Prologue*

I was examining a collection of old shepherd's crooks standing up in an umbrella rack. An elderly man, tweed cap pulled down against unseasonably cold weather, presided over them. He stood back, silently letting me explore each one. I shook my head at the appeal of these simple sticks. One had a deer's foot embedded in the "turn" in the crook. The reddish tan hair was still on it, and you could pet it in the right direction. I smoothed it gently for some time, a comforting bit of fur at an unexpected moment.

I reached for another, the handle an elaborate curlicued ram's horn the color of ivory, with horizontal ruts in it, for traction, I suppose, when the ram was fighting. It must have been handsome and formidable when worn by its owner. The staff was a strapping branch with knots clearly visible. It had been shellacked a deep reddish brown and was quite long. A stately, dressy crook meant for a shepherd running in a big sheepdog trial. Then I saw the simplest one, the handle a free form duck's bill, the staff thin and reedy, on the short side and light enough to be hooked by a pinky. That would be my working crook. I continued to sift through the crooks, which were being sold to raise money for a veterans' charity sponsored by a local hospital. I finally chose seven or eight that I thought would stand me in good stead for decades longer than I would still be working sheepdogs and competing in sheepdog trials.

I had turned my back firmly on the business going on behind me. An auction of 150 working border collies was in progress at the Skipton auction house in the north of England. It was the best known of all the sheepdog auctions in the UK, was well attended, and typically attracted the best sheepdogs and the highest prices. Buyers, mostly men, and many wearing tweed caps identical to the crook purveyor's, were crowded around a huge grassy corral, six or seven deep, following the lot numbers in their catalogues and marking off sales and prices. The auctioneer stood on a raised platform. He hummed along at "forty five hundred forty five forty five five thousand five thousand . . ." He scanned the crowd to make eye contact with several important buyers who only had to nod slightly to put in their bid.

While the bidding on a dog was going on, the seller was working the dog in the ring. Four sheep had been let out at one end, and the dog was gathering, driving, and flanking the four. The same sheep were used repeatedly and misbehaved badly, taking off for their corner whenever they got a chance to escape and refusing to be pried out no matter how hard the dog tried. But that didn't seem to bother the bidders. In a matter of seconds, the bidding often rose to the mid to high four figures, sometimes to ten or even fifteen thousand guineas. I watched as shepherds, farmers, and trialers bid huge sums for the dogs they wanted. Some were there representing foreign buyers and spent much of their time on their mobiles.

It was hard to tell how much the bidding was driven by what buyers saw in the ring and how much by what they already knew about the bloodlines, the littermates, or the dog itself. The bidding went at a dizzying pace, and I was careful to meet no one's eyes, scratch no part of my face nor raise an arm even an inch from my side lest I find myself submitting a bid. A dog I had been tempted to bid on exceeded my top price in less than a minute and was gaveled in two minutes.

I recognized a famous Welsh handler standing next to me, who didn't know me. He had just won a bid on a fairly expensive dog who had not overly impressed me. But I knew I did not know enough to evaluate the dogs with the lightning speed of these savvy handlers. I was behind the eight ball, would never get a bargain here. I hesitated, then plunged into conversation with him.

"May I ask what you saw in that dog that prompted you to bid that much on him? He seemed nice to me (I was polite!), but I didn't see anything inspirational about him. I am trying to learn to see better.... I'm not very good," I explained, lest he think me rude.

He smiled sympathetically. "I liked the way he put his head down and pushed when they refused to line out on the drive. I think he's got something."

I nodded as if I understood, but to me it didn't seem nearly enough to justify the price. The dog seemed ordinary; there was no poetry in his movement or in his eye, no breathtaking "feel" for his sheep. Much later, I decided he was probably buying what he considered an adequate dog for a student. What I didn't yet understand was that my standards were impossibly high, that I was fortunate enough to own a dog whose eye was electric, whose feel for sheep was subtle and powerful, in short, a dog who was thrilling to watch, my dog of a lifetime. "Why would anyone settle for less?" I wondered.

And therein lies the dilemma. What was clear from the bustle, the attentiveness, the whispered reactions to the dogs and the prices, was that in a tiny part of everyone's mind lay the insistent hope that one of these dogs would be that one, that special, beautiful one, the dog of a lifetime. If you have that dog, you know the hope, the excitement, the wonder of it. You know the bliss, the astonishment, the communication. You know the confidence you enjoy, the protection you feel. If you haven't had that dog, you don't know what you don't know, but you still hope for it, and you listen to the stories with curiosity, envy, and admiration. If you've had that dog and you've outlived it, you are a marked man, for you are forever hoping to get it again, knowing you cannot make that happen. I swear I can see it on certain faces, haunted by the desire for what might be given at any moment, with luck, but which can never be bought.

## Chapter 1: How It Works

By rights, I shouldn't be here. I was sitting on a camp chair, baseball cap helmet-like, blocking the glare, squinting to watch five sheep on a distant hill about to be moved, "lifted" we call it, by a border collie who had run out 700 yards to bring them down the field. I was at a sheepdog trial. Fifty handlers and their border collies were competing to drive five unbroke sheep perfectly around a challenging course. We were watching with our minds in a no-man's state, suspended between catching up with friends and scrutinizing the runs in anticipation of our own. Hoping to get a hint of where the sheep wanted to go, their behavior, and the amount of pressure our dog needed to exert to barely move the sheep. Not enough pressure and the sheep might "get ideas" and run off, too much and they might turn and fight. No matter how hard I watch, it feels different as soon as I am up. Still, I try to have a strategy for each problem I see others having.

It took me a long time to get to the point of having a strategy. It takes mental discipline to forego the pleasures of talking to handlers I don't see except at trials, take in tantalizing stories of their new dogs, planned breedings or how they've corrected a difficult problem. Instead one has to watch other runs carefully, identify the problems caused by the terrain or the sheep and decide how to handle them with the dog you are about to run, taking his strengths and weaknesses into account. I don't think well on my feet, never have. A top handler said at his clinic, "For you, as developing handlers, everything goes by during your run at 100 mph, while for me, it goes by at 25 mph." Developing strategies ahead of my run is my way of slowing it down so that I can problem-solve along the way.

The key element to a good strategy is minute observation. Your strategy may be sound, but its execution depends on close monitoring of the sheep and dog all the way around the course. Two people can look at the same run as hard as they can; only one will see, with laser vision, the dog accelerate slightly on the fetch, his last stride slightly faster than the previous. This will cause the sheep to gain speed until they are barreling down the field, missing panels and the turn around the post. Catching that nanosecond when the dog first speeds up may be the difference between winning and retiring.

I have asked top handlers, who buy expensive dogs off the internet with a brief phone call after seeing a two-minute video, what they saw. "I saw something in the way he turned his sheep just there at that moment that I liked." The split-second decision to stop, steady or flank your dog, just when everything seems to be going right, is the work of champions. They proactively make subtle corrections before the sheep go offline by watching these minute changes, while the beginner is afraid to rock the boat as long as everything is going fine. By the time they see it is going wrong, it is too late.

It has been said that this is the only sport that involves a person and two different animal species, sheep and dogs. It is a complicated triangle, with each player affecting the other two. That is what is so hard to understand at high speed. Though meticulous training is essential, it is never sufficient. There is always an unknown chemical reaction between sheep, dog and yourself at the trial that can help or hurt you.

A talented dog can help you problem-solve these new situations imperceptibly. You may never even catch on to what your dog did to enhance your run. Or the reverse. Certain sheep met at a trial can agitate a dog in ways never seen during training. It is what makes working border collies on sheep so mysterious and so addictive. To make the dynamic even more complicated, as you are getting to know your dog and learning how to handle him at a trial, he is also evolving. As he matures and gains confidence, his ability to handle difficult sheep is improving, so you can gradually lessen control, cede him more responsibility, strengthen the partnership. Conversely, as he gains confidence, he wants to wrest control from you when he should not, so you have to exercise more control than formerly. Both are matters of judgement.

But the main thing that drives you on in this most difficult sport is your admiration, love and gratitude for your magnificent animal. We are each, as we watch, besotted with our own dog. We forget his flaws for the moment and are proud of his skills, his intelligence, his heroism, his sheep sense, his talent. Each new trial is an opportunity to hone skills and show off our champions.

Handlers talk about their dogs' loyalty in heroic terms. One says, "She would stop breathing if I asked her to." A famous handler says of his Supreme Champion, "He would walk through a wall for me." A friend says about her dog King, a son of my own champion,

Gus, "He is my world. He would put sheep on the moon if I asked him to." This is a story of one dog's talent and beauty, but also of his flaws. It is a story of a pilgrimage toward understanding—of my dog, the sport, myself. It describes my infatuation with his magnificent talent and the difficult effort to see him whole.

At this moment I was watching a friend's dog on the course. This dog's problem was, he was a "wing-wanger." The optimal dog would "flank" (circle his sheep) effortlessly when asked but would otherwise walk with a slow crouch into his sheep with torpedo-like directness, his eye fixed and cold, signaling no quarter. But this one pushed his sheep by "overflanking" (pushing his sheep first to one side, then the other in a series of quick mini gathers) until the sheep—heavy range ewes who don't like sudden changes in direction—balked in consternation, wheeled and turned on the dog. The lead ewe might use her head as a weapon, fling it or bring it down like a hammer on the dog, face him off and push him back. Once this standoff occurred, at 500 yards away, you couldn't help your dog. He might get stuck, be unable to move the packet any farther or "grip" (bite) that sheep in self-defense. Grips not taken strictly on the nose, then quickly released, were cause for disqualification by the judge. A dog could defend himself but could not take advantage.

My friend was lucky. Her dog stood his ground while the sheep faced him off. Then they decided they wouldn't fight; instead they turned and trotted forward. Crisis averted until the next time he "got in their eye" (overflanked so far that he caught their eye, and they faced him off).

It was a beautiful day, by some people's lights, the California sun shining on rolling hills still green from a deluge a week before. John Muir, who wrote famously about California nature, spoke of the rain that comes on suddenly, no temperature drop or threatening wind, that falls steadily without drama for several days, then vanishes. Temperatures stay mild, in the 50s or 60s as if they don't know it's raining. Then relentless sun again.

This field was a specially blessed place. A ranch of thousands of acres, the trial host promised a different venue each year. That way, repeat trialers never had an advantage the following year. Spotting your sheep at 700 yards is a special talent in a dog. Border collies have long memories. A dog that's run a course even once will probably remember where the sheep were set and have a leg up on spotting them the next year. This particular field rose high above a tributary of the Sacramento River. A tug labored along it, while a small sailboat, sail sprung, moved quickly by. It felt like a snapshot from a Dutch master, and the sun gave the sail density and the air an almost Van Gogh-like swimming quality.

My own run was adequate, nothing more. Gus runs with what is called "tension." In this sport, informed practitioners don't psychologize it, don't say "it's anxiety about moving, finding, holding his sheep" or, "he has anxiety, therefore he's not a confident dog." They just say "he runs with tension." This means that at home, he will eat up ground running out in a beautiful arc either side of his sheep, pause behind and pick them up gently and subtly, then tend them all the way down the field, tucking them in, bending solicitously toward them, delivering them to his shepherd with care. People who work dogs with me who see it might watch it in silence or exclaim over the gentle beauty of it. But at a trial, with unfamiliar sheep, he is trembling at the post like a diesel engine, scooting to set up first to my left then my right, aching to be gone. Not listening.

When he gets to the top and the sheep start to move, so does he. Pushing fast, he has them running. I blow a steady command, no response. I yell a warning "Gus" and get a slight slowing. He is in constant motion. By the time they are at my feet and ready to start the drive, they are doing anything to avoid him.

Today, he gives me something, a decent fetch, not upsetting his sheep. I get hold of him, screw him down as he marches his sheep through the first drive panel and across to the second (the "cross-drive" panel). Cross-drive panels are notoriously difficult to negotiate. This one is at an odd angle, an optical illusion. The inside panel is useless, pointed straight at me. I try to feel whether he has brought the sheep below or above the inside panel. The best handler of the day brakes his dog hard at this point, nudges his sheep just far enough to see whether their noses break the plane below or above. If below, he still has a chance to flank his dog and push his sheep up to make the panel. That's at least five points, the difference between placing and not. That is also control I do not have today. We miss it low.

Once we've missed it, there is no going back; he turns his sheep down toward me and the shed ring. The shed is the first time the handler is allowed to leave the post, to enter the shed ring. The shed demonstrates the dog's courage and training. It requires him to rush through a small hole that opens up suddenly in a tight-knit group of sheep, separate the ones indicated by the handler, and walk them away. Today we have four sheep and must take the last two "on the head." This means that I make a hole between the first two and the last two, all facing one way. On my call-in of "Gus, this!" he gallops into the hole, turns to face the last two head to head, and drives them away. Judge calls "ok" when the dog has demonstrated control of the two. Since sheep long to flock, holding some off from the others demonstrates the dog's power. Once a judge waited what seemed an eternity before he accepted my shed. Asked later why he waited so long, he responded, "Because your dog was only looking at one sheep, not both."

    I look at my watch. We still have four minutes, enough time to really work at the pen, the last element. We have started to practice this, my weakest skill, with determination. Gus knows to approach the pen cautiously. He brings our sheep slowly to the mouth, while I try to turn each head into the pen using my crook. Sheep go where their heads go. As they turn, I take a step forward: at the pen "never give up ground you've won" I have learned. The ewe at the far side has turned her head outside the pen on Gus's side. I have to hold the rope attached to the pen gate, am too far away to turn her head with my crook. She could bolt out if I don't flank my dog to block her. But if he overflanks, the sheep could turn and bolt out my side; the result is a long regather and restart. I watch the sheep and say, "Gus" without looking at him. It is enough to say his name; he knows what to do. The sheep's head turns slightly back inside the pen; he's blocked her.

I look at the faces of the ewes. They are nervous, licking their mouths, heads held abnormally high, eyes busy. I wait a few seconds for them to calm before pushing again. I relax my body, since they read it better than I do. I exhale, let my belly protrude and shoulders sag, go still and wait. Then I straighten up, stand tall and walk forward; they go in slowly. I tighten the rope, pull the gate around, block the opening with my body and close the gate. I am happy. We have done well enough to place in the points.

*Training and Its Vicissitudes*

Two days later, at home, I am still aggravated by Gus's tension in our second run. A fiasco, he galloped his sheep down the fetch line and around the course. It is not supposed to be this way. As they get older, the dogs are supposed to settle down, work more slowly and give the handler the control and flexibility he needs to make the obstacles. But Gus's tension seems to be rising. He was especially pushy at the lift and fetch, where the dog first makes contact with the sheep; disturbing his sheep at the lift affects the rest of the run. If he lifts gently, the sheep will calm and trust him. If he lifts hard, they might run, and I would lose control. His pushiness forces me to scream "lie down" repeatedly in a rising pitch, which he ignores. I sound angry and out-of-control. There is nothing worse than coming off the field ashamed of how you've spoken to your dog. I've seen the looks other handlers exchange when an angry handler is at the post. I don't know whether I'll ever be able to control him.

I struggled with my panicked feelings at his pushiness. I didn't understand why he did it or how to fix it.

I saw his tension as a fault that was extraneous, unnecessary. If only he could do everything he did for me, but without the tension! I thought back to a Nevada trial which featured wild sheep. The runs at that trial were chaotic, and, as is said in such cases, "the sheep won." My current trainer, a person of quiet wisdom, had been at the top of the field all day, setting out groups of five sheep for each handler's run. She took the five out of a corral holding the entire flock, the setout pen. She had seen at close range every dog try to gather his sheep and fetch them down the field, had seen many fail. What made this particular lift so difficult, the judge remarked later, was that the setout pen was positioned at a full right angle to the spot where the dog has first contact with his sheep. Dogs generally expect to come in from behind and nudge the sheep forward. But when the sheep bolt hard right to the setout pen when the dog approaches, trying to rejoin the flock for safety, the dogs are not ready for it.

At the handlers' dinner that evening she showed me a video she had taken on her phone of Gus lifting his sheep. As he arrives at the top of the field and comes in from behind, they scatter and bolt right as had other groups. I see what I could not see from the post. Gus, working independently, swerves and wheels to round up first one ewe, then another. He flanks back and forth at a frantic pace to prevent them from escaping, while they split and try to beat him back to the setout pen. Finally, he masters them and begins the fetch downfield at a run. I can be heard from the post yelling "stead-y!," which he ignores. I'm distressed by the video and say, "He looks completely out of control!" She answers pointedly, "He brought them down the field. Many dogs did not." Then it was that I started to realize the force field, the whirlwind, at work when Gus bent wild sheep to his will and fetched them to me. Perhaps tension might be the price I paid for his heroic feats.

I relive all this on the way out to train. In the car my friend Anne calls. She reads my mind and gives me a stern lecture about what a talented dog Gus is. "Vicky," she admonishes, "he is a beautiful dog." By the end of the call, she has me in a Zen-like state of heightened awareness and self-confidence. I can help restore him and calm myself.

I have an idea. I decide to work my very heavy unbroke range sheep in my arena, as they are still too wild to work in an open field. We take three and Gus pushes them through the gate into the arena. They are already fighting and balking. His head comes down. Now he is controlling them with his eye, addressing each one in turn to force them through the gate. He places each foot carefully, watching them intently. He holds them with the power of his eye. No need to hound him for a steady here; these ewes are more likely to turn on him than run from him. He drives them around the arena, momentarily averting his gaze to take the pressure off them and allow them an escape route forward, where I want them to go. Then he moves back to pure push, head down like a steam shovel, implacable. They read him perfectly, speeding up when he feints off and releases them, slowing when he overtly bosses. His feel for sheep is perfection itself, my voice no more than a whisper.

We try to pen, first time ever with these new ewes. We inch along on either side of the pen to try to funnel them in. Gus overflanks before I can stop him; the sheep turn and run out of pen mouth on my side. He gets them back, we push together, they go in. He is breathing hard from the concentration. It's not hot, and he has barely had to move. I praise him in gratitude. This could have been a trial pen, sheep are that tough. But together we worked it out, each did our part. He gives me a huge, toothy grin of pleasure at the praise and gets in the water to cool down his mind. Only now do I marvel at his talent, his sheep sense, his work ethic, his courage. I think now he is the best dog I have ever had, will ever have. Tomorrow this might all change.

My friends from graduate school cannot get over the image of me driving a half-ton Ford diesel, pulling a trailerful of sheep. They see wifebeaters somehow involved. Pulling a trailer was certainly not part of the suburban culture I grew up in, where dogs were pets and livestock unknown. Many handlers in the west came to working border collies from riding horses, so they understand the mentality of prey animals—horses and sheep—and predators—dogs—much better than I do. I am a neophyte in this sheepdog culture in so many ways and cannot shake off that uncomfortable feeling, though I strive for understanding.

Everyone in this sport who can, trailers sheep out to remote areas where they can practice 500 yard outruns or watch their dog drive sheep 300 yards away across the side of a hill, correcting the line by himself, without a word from the handler. Silently watching your dog drive peacefully, effortlessly, correctly on his own for long moments is one of the true pleasures of the sport. He forgets about you, though he still has one ear cocked for your command, head and tail come down, he focuses solely on the job at hand. He doesn't rush or take advantage, he sorts out small problems in the terrain that might bother the sheep, slowing and giving them time to cross a difficult patch, but the invisible magnet between him and them never weakens. He controls them with his eye rather than his body. Rarely does a dog look more beautiful than when concentrated on his task, his instinct and nature working in harmony with the ideals of good stockmanship.

A top handler has said, "*every whistle feels like a correction to a dog,*" the point being, to build confidence in your dog, less is more. The more you command and control, the more you intervene between your dog and his instincts. These instincts are the source of your dog's power and desire to work and must be respected and nourished. A creative handler strives to provide the conditions under which a dog works his sheep correctly on his own. Achieving that state is its own strange high that energizes and refreshes.

One of the first dogs I ever had was very difficult for me to start. A friend recommended a fellow up north who had a good reputation. He would later become one of the best handlers in the US and my trainer for a time. He obligingly took my dog for training. After a couple of months I called him for a progress report. He was noncommittal, hadn't really taken the dog's measure yet. I asked him how he trained. After a pause he drawled, "I put 'em in situations."

I didn't understand this at the time. Now, that is exactly what I do: put them in a "situation" which is set up to be difficult and then help them fix it, if they need help. You let the sheep do something you know they want to do, like run, and watch what the dog does. Does he flank around, get in front of them, to stop them bravely? Does he chase and grip, scattering them? Does he down himself flat to the ground and stare at them without moving. Does he cast out so far that he is almost running away and never faces them in order to turn them back? These various responses tell you a lot about the dog's courage and talent.

Even more importantly, by putting the dog in situations, you are letting him experience his sheep, giving him a chance to respond. You are not molding and dominating him from the git-go, rather giving him permission to respond with everything he has. If he shows you something good here, you can build on it, shape it, help him unlock his genetic capability rather than imposing a rote progression of "skills" on him. If you have the good fortune to work with a talented dog, you are on safe ground to give him increasing amounts of responsibility. You trust him. You and he have a common task. You are not training him; you and he are in a partnership, a relationship. You are putting your heads together to find a means to achieve a necessary solution involving your stock. At its best, this is a creative process, filled with daily miracles of communication and mutual mind reading. Each of you modifies the other's practices. People sometimes call this type of border collie an "honest" dog.

And that is why, when trialers get together and find themselves with extra time on their hands, they have "silent gather" competitions, where the dogs work with *no commands allowed*. Which dog brings the sheep down with the minutest, subtlest corrections, achieving a perfectly straight line? Who has the most natural pace, meshing with his sheep, tending the line, urging his sheep on without pushing them into a sloppy canter? In short, which dog understands on his own the best way to handle these particular sheep because his handler has helped him to discover it?

But training is complicated, and different needs require a different mix of instinct and control. Shepherding has different requirements from trialing. Here is a Cumbrian shepherdess describing how her work calls for a dog with a toughness and independence not suited to the trial field. Her six year-old "work horse":

> does not do trials anymore, as I get only frustrated fighting over who runs who! You can tell him what to do but he decides how. And luckily he has a very good work brain so I've finally agreed to his terms and everyone's happy and jobs get done without a fuss. Yeh . . . and when my main dog died in an accident, he was just a teenager, far from being ready for dogging killer sheep, but I had to earn money. So he learned to "survive" his own way and had to be very tough and too much. So it is my fault really that today he doesn't take instructions easily, and I appreciate him so much that he got us through that period and we had food on the table! It's me who owes him, and he is perfect the way he is. And, oh yes, he will never be leaving my side.

I had some very good dogs before Gus. They were strong, had beautiful eye, were fleet and athletic, but I had not broken the species barrier yet and could not enter their minds. I had not meshed with them as I came to do with Gus. My training, or lack thereof, was most certainly the reason. Less benign even than a blank slate, I was anxious, peremptory, authoritarian. I had almost no tools and no understanding at all.

I remember running Gwynnie, a handsome black-and-white girl, Canadian bred, at a trial in Arizona. She was exhibiting her worst qualities: she was pouty and stubborn. Her disobedience frustrated me, and it showed in my angry tone during my run. A top handler whom I hardly knew came over to chat afterwards. He agreed her lines did have a lot of poutiness in them. But, he said, to get my dog to do something she doesn't like, like lying down, I need to give her something fun to do after that. I looked at him, baffled. "What's fun for a dog?" I asked. I could see him recalibrating my level of ignorance.

He hesitated, "well, a flank, for instance. Dogs love to flank." What he actually meant, I believe, is that a flank is a mini-gather. "Gathering" (casting out in a wide arc around sheep who are some distance away and fetching them to the handler) is the instinctual basis of all a collie's skills, and dogs relax when gathering. After you ask the dog for something counter-intuitive, like lying down, give them a flank, since it satisfies their instinct. But it would be years before I understood that.

I wore my ignorance badly. I was immobilized by my lack of tools and understanding. And not all trainers could explain the why behind their instructions. Instead they gave you a set of directions—"walk over here (steering you by your elbow), blow your dog down at the top, shush your dog around right there, take one step forward, now say nothing." They didn't explain the reasons for their directions. I learned some things, but not enough to understand and fix a problem on my own. While you were working with them, you saw talents in your dog you never saw before. But you left as ignorant as you came, with nothing to build on at home.

Finally, I met someone who talked in complete paragraphs, used general principles to introduce the problem we were working on, and followed it up with well-designed training exercises. We went from the very basic—how to correct a dog without his becoming sour—to the very subtle. She said of her exercises that I should practice them at home, but that my own creative understanding would soon enable me to innovate and advance. And, indeed, that is what happened.

But I did not meet her until Gus was six. There was another influence that helped me see better, drop my authoritarian tendency and realize that training was a conversation between dog and handler. And that influence was Gus himself.

## Gus

Shortly after I bought him and he had returned from a few months of basic training, I took him out with my two Open dogs for a morning of training. I had worked them in a big field and was walking Gus back to the truck on leash, as he was still too new to let loose. My Open dog, Daisy, was driving the sheep back to the trailer ahead of me. Before I knew it, she had turned the sheep around and was fetching them back to me, holding them to me. I should have realized she would do this; it is what working border collies do naturally. In the process, she was driving the sheep straight into Gus's face, who walked beside me on leash.

The transformation in him was startling. He geared down from a nonchalant trot to a crouchy, careful walk, his head dropping low and jutting forward as he paused and swept each face in the flock with his eye, studying each one, attempting to turn them back on Daisy. His eye was electric and seemed to engulf his sheep; he held them with his eye. The leash went slack. He slowed, lifted each foot and placed it with deliberation as he assessed his stock and took their measure. He worked stealthily so as not to upset them. His feel for sheep was powerful, a thing of wonder. His concentration, his judgement and his care were a revelation to me, and a deep sense of respect and curiosity about him welled up in me. I could not take my eyes off him. He had not a shred of fear before the sheep, only the desire to mesmerize them with his eye and so control them. Until that moment I had never felt the power of a dog's eye as I did then. The phrase often used about good dogs—"quiet power"—came to mind.

In those early months of training Gus and getting to know him, he performed some amazing feats for me. I quickly lengthened his "outrun" (casting out wide enough to gather sheep so that they don't move until the dog lifts them) which I could see was perfectly pear-shaped, correct both left and right, and reliable every time. He cast wide and beautifully deep at the top, but was never out of contact, as his drive to reach his sheep was strong. He ran out with purpose. A humble 150 yard outrun quickly grew to a magisterial 400 yards.

His sheep-spotting skill was unerring. He always spotted all the sheep on the field and followed them with his eye. I worked in a huge field owned by the local utility. I had been lucky enough to gain permission from the rancher who leased it for cattle grazing to trailer my sheep out and work my dogs there. Daringly, though I was only a beginning Open handler, I had imported some beautiful Rambouillet range ewes from Utah. They were culls from a finely bred flock usually sold as foundation stock. They were huge and could be wild.

One day, for no reason I could fathom, a single ewe took off from the flock, ran all the way downfield, and joined a large herd of the rancher's black angus cattle. She embedded herself in the midst of the herd. I was distraught, not sure I could make any of my dogs understand how to spot her and get her back. Which dog should I send? My two Open dogs were lying down, looking at nothing in particular. I looked at Gus. He was quite a bit younger and far less experienced than my Open dogs. But he had seen the ewe leave and was staring at her as she cantered down the field. She was by now at least 400 yards away.

I stood directly facing the escaping ewe, took one step forward, and said "Gus, away" (the command to run out to the right). He took off with purpose, widened out as he approached her, and came in deep behind her. I laid him down. The cattle were drifting slowly sideways and, after a minute, had passed the ewe, leaving her exposed. I asked him to walk up. He walked in on her, leaned toward her, teased her away from the cows and started fetching her back to me. His art as he moved her astonished me. He stayed far behind her, head down, watching her and guiding her from behind, never closing the gap between them. They each maintained a slow trot. Whenever she deviated from the line, he floated out sideways, moving just far enough into her peripheral vision to encourage her back online. He didn't boss or threaten; he cajoled and was solicitous. They came on smoothly, as if linked by invisible magnets, flowing together as if on two connected railcars.

I watched in silence. He brought her to my feet. He must have been three by then, I'm not sure. The control, his restraint, the peacefulness of it all, the correctness of the line, his understanding of the task, were dazzling. What would I have done without him? Lost a sheep, who might have ended up running toward the local airport behind us, causing havoc, perhaps causing me to lose access to this beautiful place? I was grateful to him and impressed with his sense of responsibility, his confidence and his maturity.

Feeling as though we could do anything together, I began to be more creative about our routines. I was still quite ignorant about training, but I experimented. I put a "look back" command on him when he was still very young, and, as a result, to this day his look back is utterly reliable. (The look back command asks the dog to leave the sheep he is working, turn 180 degrees and run out to look for a second group, whether he can see them or not.) I started working with two groups of sheep on the field, one group to work, the other to stand somewhere on the field to create "pressure" (the desire of a group of sheep to run—to safety, food, to rejoin the rest of the flock—which the dog must be strong enough to prevent). Sometimes the working group got too close to the standing group and tried to merge with them. I could always direct Gus to flank around quickly, slip in between and catch the working group before they merged by turning my body toward them and indicating, "this, this!"

Or the standing group would decide to run to the working group. Then I would tell him "look back!" He would turn 180 degrees and walk up on the flock barreling toward him, boldly cut them off and march them back to their spot. He understood these tasks immediately. Perhaps innately, perhaps because of his exceptional eyesight, or perhaps because of this early training with multiple groups on the field, he has always known where all the sheep are on any field and is ready for them when it is his turn to work. That is why only he, and neither of my Open dogs, could have retrieved the single ewe that struck out for the cattle.

Over his working life, he continued to reveal aspects of his vast talent. He was an infallible sheep spotter, no matter how far away the sheep were set. He would scan the horizon in a wide arc until he saw his sheep, then freeze his gaze on them and lower into a crouch until he was sent. His cast was perfect both left and right. He was a natural at shedding, could fit himself into a tight hole and rush in on the cue of "Gus, this!" When he was still quite young, at a trial in Colorado, the judge exclaimed over his shed, "That dog helped you without your saying a word!" I tucked that away with pride. His hearing was so good, I had actually given him one or two verbal commands, but in such a low voice it was all but inaudible to anyone else. But he was right; Gus understood the shedding task, and repositioned himself as I moved my body, ready to run in when the hole opened up.

Gus was slow to mature and slow to reveal his talent. This is not uncommon. When I got him, I saw nothing of it, and neither did trainers with much more knowledge than I possessed. He was sold by a handler who had too many young dogs and thought he might be too soft to handle stroppy range sheep. Once I got him, a friend tried to start him, but he ran under the trailer at one soft flick of her flag and wouldn't come out even though sheep were standing close by. I finally decided to send him away to a trainer who got him going nicely, but who also saw little talent. When I called to ask how he was doing and what he was like, the answer came back, "Nah-h, he's nothing special. But he seems to be a natural penner." Indeed, he was. Though *I* didn't learn how to pen reliably for years, *he* knew how to early on. Once I learned, I can hardly remember a pen after that that we missed over the rest of his trialing life.

How did it happen that no task was too difficult for this "nothing special" dog? How did this "nothing special" dog become everything to me? People hypothesize the existence of special chemistry between dog and handler that creates this relationship as the dog matures and as they grow together. Perhaps that is how it happened. I continue to believe it was all him.

At home his glad spirit shone through. He was an easy, happy boy, would sigh with contentment as he curled up on the sofa between my husband and me at the end of a day. He enjoyed life to the fullest. When I invited him onto the bed for a belly rub or a cuddle, he would lie next to me and look at me over his shoulder with his big smile and the most knowing eyes I have ever seen on a dog. He drank you in. You could gaze into his warm brown eyes for some time; he did not interpret it as aggression. In his almond-shaped eyes, I saw the Vermeer Girl with a Turban, with the same expressive pools that drew one in.

He knew how to cuddle, how to fit his big, barrel shaped torso into your side, fling his front paws around you and press his head next to yours, close and still. And so we would sit, cheek to cheek, comforted by each other. He had an innate need to connect and communicate. I attributed some of this to the family he was raised with before he came to us; they told of feeding him pizza crusts on the couch while watching TV. Dogs I've had that were raised only in outdoor kennels sat stiffly on the bed, enjoying the intimacy more in the thought than in the deed.

Gus was very verbal, would grunt and groan with pleasure over many things—a belly rub, petting of any kind, getting ready to go out to sheep. At belly rubs, he would torque his head at an impossible angle and stretch a paw upward, but otherwise not move for fear of curtailing one of his greatest pleasures. His eyes would close, and his groans were deep, rhythmic and fulsome. It was seductive; how could one end this routine that sent him into ecstasy? He had a series of grunts and groans for displeasure, too, could mewl at length or bark demandingly if dinner didn't appear soon enough. Then he would make a show of marching into the kitchen, head turned back to see whether I was following. Once at an outdoor evening meal at a trial, I put him in a crate just as dinner was served. He gave a human sigh of exasperation at being locked in a crate when potential admirers were present and food was being served.

He is a handsome boy, vital and bristling with good health. He has ears like a horse, curved on the outside, straight on the inside, sticking straight up when there is something of interest—livestock, a strange noise, any sound or word coming from me, a snap of my fingers, which might mean hop up in the truck, stop that scratching, or pay attention, I'm leaving the room. He has a craggy, masculine head with a pronounced stop, slightly puffy cheeks and a blunt, not foxy nose. His head is broad and big, the blunt nose adding to the overall impression of masculinity. The sooty bits on the bridge of his nose look, up close, like a herringbone pattern of black and white, gray from farther away. His build is stocky, bulldog-like, front legs akimbo, and his chest is deep and broad, evidence of his massive endurance and lung capacity. His legs are short; he stands low to the ground. He has a thick, sooty ruff, looking almost ticked, and a luxurious shining coat. He keeps himself fastidiously clean, as men do who deservedly pride themselves on their good looks, and smells faintly and pleasantly of warm earth.

    He is white-factored, which has limited his breeding opportunities, but when bred to a dark bitch, he has turned out very dark progeny. The black of his fur is pitch black, shiny, gleaming and smooth to the touch. His fur grew perfectly around his toes; he never had the unsightly, straggly fur that grows an inch over the front feet—like ear-hair in men. But his most distinctive markings are the naughty spots, the mottle everywhere, belly, chest, beneath his chin, front and back legs, toes. It is a bit shocking until you grow used to it and no longer regard it as strange. His coat is so dense, I can't remember when I started thinking of it as a lynx coat.

## A Handling Disappointment

I drove sixteen hours to an out of state trial I'd never been to. I knew nothing of the field, the sheep or the judge. The sheep were from a commercial flock, rather than the wild range ewes featured at the most prestigious western trials, like Meeker and Soldier Hollow, sheep that one could not get near and who feared humans fully as much as dogs. Meeker sheep spend the winter in huge bands in the mountains fighting off cougar and coyotes, and when they agree to be lifted and driven down the trial field by a border collie, they are strutting, ripped, and confident enough to send a beginning Open handler back to his car and on his way home without ever running his dog. No, these sheep had seen dogs when moved in large lots and were used to pens and people.

Two of the five sheep wore collars (in this case yellow crime scene tape), three did not. The handler had to shed off two of the three unmarked sheep and "single" (separate a single sheep from one of the two marked ones). Once a marked sheep figured out you were after her, she sensed persecution and burrowed her head deep into the middle of the packet. It was an art to tease her out. One had to be calm and work crisply but without undue insistence and certainly not desperation, all while the clock was ticking.

There were several Californians there. Though we were not close, we were always friendly, and here we hung together, discussing the sheep and runs. We did not know the local handlers well. I for one was only moderately impressed with their performances. Some were loud, their dogs disobeyed and lines were not straight. Handlers set up the shed incorrectly, so that they, not the dog, stood on the pressure side (where the sheep most wanted to run) and so were unable to stop the sheep from running out of the ring before the shed was complete, an expensive mistake. I did not see a lot of beauty here.

A few runs before mine I started studying the course. The setout pen was to the right of where the sheep were being set. The sheep would have a strong "draw" or desire to run sideways to rejoin their friends in the setout pen if the dog did not take charge. For full points, the dog's first contact with the sheep, the "lift," should move the sheep straight forward toward the handler. Sideways movement is penalized. I assumed most handlers would send their dogs to the right, to block the sideways pressure to the pen. As I watched, someone unbelievably sent left. The sheep easily beat the dog back to the pens. Unable to peel his sheep off the fence, he retired. Next handler up, I watched the setout crew encourage the sheep to come forward onto the hay, then back away warily and in concert, forming an arc behind the sheep. Good setout crew! When they stopped moving, I would send my dog.

Gus ran out to the right and steadied to my whistle as he lifted. As expected, his sheep veered to the right. I saw his head pop around them as he fought to push them back online. I steadied him hard, as they were coming too fast for my liking. His sheep were now right online, and his pace slowed just a tad. Now, closer to me, he would listen better. I slowed him again to a fast walk, his sheep slipped through the fetch gates, rounded the post and started the drive. But then without warning, they bolted straight up the field for several yards, quite offline. I flanked him, steadied him again, and they walked quietly through the driveaway panels. On the cross drive they gathered speed, as other packets had, through no fault of the dog. But as a famous Scottish handler had pointed out to me somewhat tartly many years before, you can't make panels if your dog is pushing them too fast. Now, with sheep at a full run, I had to flank Gus just enough to straighten them out and aim them toward the panel. I flanked him, they went low. I had missed it, could not see where the path through was.

They turned the panel wide, still more points off. I tried to brake him quite hard going into the shed ring. If they run in, chances are they will run right out the other side, half the shed points lost before we'd even started. He walked, they walked into the ring. These ewes were hard to sort. Milling them to get two unmarked ones made them want to run out of the ring. I finally got two off, Gus shot through at a weird angle, but we made it. I ran to the pen. Gus brought them slowly and nudged them toward the pen mouth. We waited a few beats, then squeezed them forward. They crowded the mouth of the pen, one head pointing out Gus's side. I said "Gus" in a low voice, and he flanked to tuck it back in. He knew what I needed; I only had to say his name. I waited. Heads started to look into the pen; one took a step in. I stood tall and pushed behind the others; they all walked in. Just as I shut the gate, time was called, so I failed the try at the pen.

I praised Gus, put him in the water trough, and started mentally calculating my score. I try to be fairly hard on myself and realistic, to face facts and avoid shock later, and also to see how well the judge's view accords with my own. In the intense concentration, one often forgets certain bobbles or doesn't notice what caused them. Your sheep suddenly bolt, taking you by surprise. What you did not see is that your dog got up too fast, rashly took two quick steps toward the sheep, and sent them running. All you know is that your run suddenly went off the rails. These mistakes can be recalled, albeit painfully, if you study the judge's markup.

I went over to the board. My score was so low, it jolted my stomach. I felt as if I'd been slapped. It felt disrespectful, rude. And in areas where we are almost universally successful. As mentioned, Gus is a natural outrunner; it is just part of his makeup. Nevertheless, four off the outrun, then seven off the lift. In my experience, seven off the lift means the sheep have run straight back, over the dog, or have practically left the field. Mine went some yards sideways, then Gus straightened them out by himself. Something was amiss here.

I started watching the runs more carefully, grading them myself, then comparing my score with the board. Hmm, the next run, sheep ran sideways quite far at the lift, three off. Judging is certainly subjective, but fairly quickly one can tell if the judge is being two things: consistent and nuanced. These two qualities express most of what one wants in a judge. Ideally, you should know your dog and your run well enough not to be surprised, sometimes even feel relief that some of the good parts you forgot did not go unappreciated even as the bad parts were penalized. The first thing I look for is that a judge is judging each part of your run with an open mind. Even if your outrun and lift are poor, if you have a sensational fetch, straight down and through the panels, the judge should switch gears and give you credit for it. I look at the horizontal, i.e. my score breakdown, but also at the vertical. If I got 2 points off my pen, which I think was an excellent pen, did anyone do better than that? If not, then that is fair. That is consistent. Raw scores matter less than the correct rank ordering of the runs. If you can say that the right dogs were rewarded, judges have done their work.

Judging is not an easy job. A judge must concentrate eight to ten hours a day, two to four days in a row and never let his mind wander. Really good judges know what the issues will be on the course and will tailor their judging to the hardships to be overcome. If the sheep are slow moving, older, canny ewes, who might not respect the dog, judges may allow the dogs to grip their sheep on the nose, if challenged, without being disqualified. Or they may allow it day one and not day two, when the sheep have become more "broke." A good judge knows when a bobble is the dog's fault, the handler's fault, or the sheep's fault, and will point accordingly. A good judge's sympathies lie with the dog, and his honest effort will be appreciated. A good judge comes out of the judging box at the end of the day and asks, "Who won?" He has focused so much on the individual elements of each run that he has not kept track of total scores, does not know where the "big hats" came out, has not let that influence his judging.

With a good judge, you don't come away feeling cheated or dissed, though you might end up very far down the rankings. Today, I concluded, California handlers were not popular here. Other handlers, usually less outspoken than I, articulated this before I had a chance to. At the end of two days, feeling demoralized, I went home, vowing to shake off this experience and work as hard as I could on my handling.

## *Training the Pup*

I muse as I drive inland to train the dogs. It is a time I use to formulate a lesson plan, just as I did when I taught freshman English. Today, I think I will shed with my pup, Zac. In a shed, which is an Open class element, handler and dog stand on opposite sides of the sheep and together string them out. Handler turns towards the last few and cries, "This!" to the dog. That hole and that body cue are the dog's signal to rush through the middle of the sheep, cut off the ones indicated, turn them and drive them away from the others. Today we start with all fifteen of my rambouillets. I make a hole and step toward 8 or so. "This!" I indicate. Zac barrels through—"Good boy!"—then I ask him to walk the eight away. The discards canter off to a safe distance.

He looks back at the discards, hesitant to let go of them. I take one more step toward the eight and repeat, "this!" Reassured, he lets the others go and drives the eight for a bit. As he brings them back, I ask for another shed. In this one, I want him not so much to cut some off as to guard his side, let go the ones I indicate. I want him to understand it is perfectly fine, when I tell him, to let sheep go. We do this a few times until he has only two sheep left from the whole flock. Groups of two and three discarded sheep are strewn about the field.

Perfect time to practice driving! Sheep attract sheep, so it won't be a simple task to get behind his sheep and go. No, these two ewes feel vulnerable separated from the others. Each group they near during the drive will be a magnet for them, and Zac will have to adjust his body to keep them from rejoining. I wait to see what he will do in this "situation."

As he nears the first group of discards, his two sheep begin to move to the right, hoping to join up. Imperceptibly, feeling their intent, he sidles to the right. *He was correcting the line by himself!* With no commands from me, he understood that he was to drive his sheep in a straight line and was adjusting his body to prevent the sheep from curving offline. Talented boy! Don't get that too often!

I now want to bring the two sheep back to me and realize I need to whistle him around 180 degrees to reverse direction. Sending him left around would be more difficult, since most of the discards were to his right, and his two sheep would try to run to them once he moved out of the way. This is called an off-pressure flank, since I am asking him now not to hold the pressure (the direction the sheep want to run), but instead to release it by flanking the opposite way. He runs the risk that he will lose his sheep to the right. But sometimes this is what must be done, either in trial or in farm work, and if a dog constantly occupies the pressure side, he can become inflexible and hard to maneuver.

I ask for the left flank. He hesitates. He understands the risk and is not sure I am right to ask for it. We discuss it. I blow another left flank, he stops but does not take it. I wait a few long seconds, blow it again. This time he takes it and whips around more than 180 degrees to compensate for the pressure from the right. Perfect. He understands the risk, still took my command,

and within those constraints, solves it by getting around as fast as possible back onto the pressure. I was training his mind.

I call him off to much praise and let him go to water. A good day's work, each element building on the last, the situations becoming increasingly difficult, new tests and new challenges introduced. He has excelled. Time to stop.

*The Nurseries*

I decided to attend a local trial, the final one before the end of the season, in a last ditch effort to get Zac qualified for the National Nursery Finals. I had already qualified Gus for the Open class finals, but Zac had earned his first nursery leg almost by a fluke and needed only a second leg to be eligible to run in the National finals. Given his age and his particular development, I had never expected to qualify him. The age requirements for qualifying are arbitrary, but so far no one has crafted an alternative. A dog can only run in the nursery finals if his third birthday falls after June 30 of the year in which he is to run. This means a dog with a birthday just before that must stop running nursery shortly after he is two. Zac has a late June birthday, the worst possible, so he could only run in the finals the September after his second birthday. A dog turning three in July can compete against my pup. So come September, my dog might be competing against a dog who is almost a year older than he is and may have almost twice as much training. So, my expectations were properly low.

But being one of the youngest dogs in his class was not Zac's biggest problem: his outrun was. The perfect outrun is "pear-shaped." As the dog runs out and approaches his sheep, a dog with "feel" casts out naturally. His instinct is to widen out to avoid disturbing them. He feels his sheep and does not want to stray inside what some trainers call the sheep's "bubble." But Zac ran tight, with no "give" in his flank as he approached his sheep. His pace was also furious, which can disturb sheep. I had tried many ways to fix the shape and the pace, to no avail. He seemed intractable.

I was feeling relaxed as I stepped to the post with Zac. Gus had won the Open trial that day, had had a beautiful, considered fetch, one in which I hardly had to blow a whistle, his movements were so thoughtful. I was proud of him and happy to get more points on him. There could be no doubt he was now qualified for Nationals. I knew Zac was young for the nurseries. I had never had a dog run in this class before, so my feeling was that a qualifier spot was unlikely, and I would just show him off the best I could.

The outrun on this course was tricky, since there were many conflicting impacts: sending to the right cut off the biggest danger, that the sheep would run back to the set-out. However, the terrain on the right side was a hill with a considerable rise. Dogs like Zac, without a natural cast, will not kick out on a hill, but instead tighten up and go flat. This is what Zac did. I groaned inwardly, thinking of the points the judge would take off. He lifted perfectly, as is usual for him, then I laid him down again. He is young, and I have not insisted on the careful steady I ask Gus for. I don't want to discourage him at this early age by exercising too much control.

He fetched his sheep down the field as straight as a torpedo, one of his best qualities. He flanked them around the post, lined them out for the drive, then went into high gear. He became ferocious, unstoppable, missed both drive panels. My heart sank. I knew this was not going to be a qualifying run. Oh, well! Since he pushed his sheep so hard, we had more than enough time for the pen. They went right in, as they were a training flock, and the pen held no terrors for them. Mine was the last run of the class. I packed up, gathered chair, thermos, crook, dogs, and loaded everything into the car.

By this time, I figured the scores were probably posted, so I went over the board to see how badly I had missed it. There were thirteen runs, so the top three dogs would qualify. Even from several yards away, I could see the three qualified dogs, marked in red, were all at the top of the run order, so that left me out. I looked at my raw score, 50 out of a possible 90. Figured. 25 off out of a possible 30 on the drive. Yes, that seemed fair. I looked at the third dog that had qualified to see how much I had missed it by: a 49. Wait a minute! I beat the third qualifying dog by one point! My voice was tremulous as I asked the trial host to review the board. Dizzying possibilities were opening up to me. Could it be? Yes, the course director had erred, did not see my 50. I was the last dog to qualify at a trial held on the last weekend of the season. We were going to the National finals, Gus, Zac, and me!

## Training for National Finals

It is three weeks before finals, and I have a date to work Gus with my trainer, who lives 500 miles away. Zac has become injured, cannot work. He won't be able to train before the finals. I hold my head, thinking of the possibilities for humiliation with no chance to train before his run. But now the main chance is Gus. He is fit, he is beautiful, he has just turned seven. He should be at the height of his powers. As the trainer and I have discussed before, he has huge talent and a beautiful willing attitude, but his excitement and tension must be controlled. If the tense Gus shows up, we can look ridiculous. If the thoughtful, prudent Gus shows up, we can be breathtakingly beautiful.

My trainer explains that if Gus is being thoughtful, I can trust him to do what is right. But the answer is not to stop him repeatedly in order to slow him. That only frustrates him, possibly leading to a grip and a DQ. He must be taught to keep the flow but to pace, keep off, give me rounded flanks, and to give to me instead of pushing the sheep relentlessly. That is the Gus I can trust. We start with some penning work. He sheds a few off, and I steady him to prepare the approach to the pen. His pace is good, but it is all going too fast for me, and I am overly cautious. I stop him before they quite reach the pen mouth. This is a mistake, because they turn and look at him, and he has to lift them again, which increases his tension.

When the sheep are on his side of the mouth, my trainer explains, he needs to move them into the mouth of the pen. I need to step back and turn my body away, otherwise my body pressure might push the sheep onto the dog, which could cause a grip. I turn my body sideways to the sheep and open the gate a bit wider. I softly cluck a walk up. There are sheep behind him in the field, of which Gus is perfectly aware, and has positioned his body directly between our sheep and the sheep behind him. That is already a smart thing to do. But I need him to flank so that he can walk them up into the pen mouth. He doesn't really want to flank, wants to stay on the pressure. He also does not want to walk directly in their faces, wants to avoid it a tiny bit, walk into their sides. His turning his head away is like my turning my body away; both diminish pressure on the sheep. This is usually a good method for moving range sheep, but at the pen he must boss them. I ask for the flank again, sharply. He gives a beautiful, rounded flank, almost an ellipse, which does not disturb the sheep, then walks them up a bit. They turn again, mill and face me this time.

    I now tell him to *get right back, get out*! He backs up six feet or so. I now move in behind the sheep and mill them so that they turn and look into the pen. I step back, ask Gus up again. He drives them right into the mouth. I ask him to get back and flank him, to prevent the sheep "escaping" out his side, because now I slide cautiously around directly behind them, face them instead of showing them my side, stand tall and walk them into the pen. Three of the five go in, two straddle the entrance and stop. One looks side to side, thinking of bolting around me. I stop, lean backwards, pause for a few seconds. I scrape my crook back and forth on the ground in front of that sheep. I cannot make a 250 pound ewe move, but I can make it unpleasant for her to stand still. She turns, and they all walk in.

As I turn to praise Gus, I notice he has taken off around the back of the pen and is about to push the sheep out. I scold him severely for this and flank him back where he was. Too many times he has ruined my pen by diving around the back to eject them before I have closed the gate!

We start over. This time, the trainer leashes one of her dogs to the side of the pen to make it harder. We take another group of five and go again. We have now done this four to five times, with urgent discussions about whether the next move is up to me or the dog, how far to flank, is he too close, etc. I am concentrating so hard, my head hurts. We have gone through all the questions and practiced it in slow motion. It doesn't feel natural yet to me. We have schooled Gus in getting back and in giving generous flanks. Now we do it again, in real time as if at a trial; I am stretched to the brink trying to remember everything I've learned, but now I also need to be fluid and natural.

We shed off five, I leave Gus holding the sheep, open the pen gate and avert my body. I give him the soft cluck. *In one motion, he propels them boldly, watching each head, walks them almost past me and right into the mouth.* I breathe in wonder, "Look at that!" I ask him to get back, give him a slight flank, and walk into my sheep to turn their heads. They resist going into the pen much more now than before because they are frightened of the dog leashed to the side. They contemplate a bolt out of the pen. I step back, ask Gus to walk them into the mouth again. Now back to plan: I ask him to get back, give him a small flank, ask for a stand, grow tall myself and walk forward. They file in, one behind the other, hugging my side of the pen to avoid the dog. I catch Gus just before he starts for the back of the pen. I lie him down, growl at him, then flank him the opposite way he wants to go.

Trainer is pleased. She says she would not have done anything differently; it could not be done better. The image of Gus boldly walking his sheep into the mouth in one movement without any instruction from me is still on my retina. How does he know exactly what to do here after only a few repetitions? That is talent of a major kind. I briefly recall his first trainer who thought he was a natural penning dog. Now that I understood penning better, I saw it. With this coaching, I can bring out the best in this dog, show off his talent, his boldness, his prudence. If we can do this at Nationals, we will achieve something beautiful.

*National Finals*

The National Sheepdog Finals have come and gone, without our having distinguished ourselves in any slight way. The buildup was intense, Zac's injury preceding it painful, but we arrived with my feeling we could take on anything. My mind was clear, Zac had recovered sufficiently, I was proud of both dogs' talents and felt no risk of the kind of humiliation that every handler dreads: his dog won't be able to lift or shift his sheep, in short, "a weak piece of ****." But, in the end, Zac's nursery run was brief, frantic and ended with a grip at the pen. Gus's run was not much better.

Funny thing is, the range sheep on the Open course announced their strategy from the start: right after the lift, break hard to handler's left, short circuit the course and bolt to the exhaust. Run fast as you can until the dog flanks around right in your face. Anything less, you keep on running. Then and only then stop, fight him to a standstill if possible, face him off, stare him down. The dog is still 400 yards from his handler, has hardly progressed down the fetch line at all, and is one hundred yards offline to the left, so the handler can hardly see what his dog is up against. Now it's all up to the dog. If he can't walk through the stare-down and shift the five under this intense pressure, the two adversaries will stare motionless until either the judge excuses the handler for lack of progress or the dog explodes in a grip to break the tension of the mutually threatening stare. If your dog has enough courage, talent, presence, and a certain "likeability" factor that relaxes the sheep so that the dog can turn them back to the fetch line, you are greatly in luck. This far we got.

The next trap set by the sheep is at the turn around the post and the beginning of the drive. The dog is almost by definition out of position around the post, since he must be behind his sheep to "open the door" for them to move in a U-shape around the post. But the lure of the exhaust is still great—still off to the left—and as the sheep consent to go around the post, they would like to make just a half turn and sprint straight to the exhaust. The dog must slow to encourage them around the post, and a second later, speed up and hook in front of them to block their path and turn them back up the field to the drive gates.

This maneuver has always been one of our fortes. Gus can slow just enough to let them spurt in a U-turn around the post, then either boldly walk up or sprint around and cut them off and turn them up the field to the drive gates. But to avoid a standoff here, I cannot let him get nose to nose. I have to try to keep him back behind them to avoid a fight. But he over-flanks slightly, so this U-turn ends up being three steps forward, a stop, then the sheep are turned back by the over-flank. Now they are confused. One tries to bolt, but Gus controls her. Most likely every step the sheep took that retraced their path due to Gus's over-flank cost me some points. But it was better than a soul-destroying standoff.

Now came the third trick the sheep played on every handler: they seemed to agree to get on an almost perfect line, heading straight toward the drive away gates. However, as they approached the panel, they veered to the right, the very opposite way they had tried to go earlier. It seemed counterintuitive, but it was a two-step chess game. As they veered right, the handler has to take the dog off the pressure (still to the left) and flank right to keep the sheep in the lane of the drive panels. As soon as the dog vacated the pressure, the sheep veered sharply left and start running across the field, missing the panel and gaining speed. The dog is now out of position. He and his handler have been elegantly suckered. Some lost their sheep at this point and retired. Gus, who obeys with alacrity, took the vigorous flank back to the left and continued on around to head to stop the sheep, almost a 360-degree flank. We paused there, because range ewes do not like sudden changes of direction, and settled them to begin anew.

The hardest part of the drive was coming up, the cross-drive panels. The angle is always misleading, a trompe l'oeil effect where you cannot see whether you will go through, above, or below until you have committed, and it is too late. No matter how slowly we go, I cannot see it. Gus was listening to perfection. I adjusted him first to bring them lower, then higher, and slowed painfully as we neared the panel. I prayed for inspiration ("Mine, O thou Lord of Life, send my roots rain") as I whistled instructions. I lined them up the best I could, slowed Gus, and they took off high, missing the gate. I swung Gus around, he caught them and brought them down and around the bottom panel on as straight a line as he could to the shed ring.

At this point, my head was spinning. I could not quite accept how thoroughly mediocre our run had been so far. I didn't see how I could be anywhere in the winning spectrum. Shedding is one of Gus's strengths, so my object was to have perfect form, get good points for the shed, have a good finish. I calmed the sheep and took one strong step toward them. At this, they split apart as if traumatized, three headed one way, two the other. I shook my head in chagrin. I was supposed to take the last two on the head. What I didn't see was that some sheep were beige, others a clear tan. These sheep were from two separate flocks! Of course they would shed easily, too easily, from the slightest pressure. No opportunity to take two "on the head." So much for my perfect form. We made an insubstantial run at the pen before time was called. I steeled myself for the score. I so wanted it to be over 100. This is why good handlers say they would prefer to grip out and DQ, rather than stay for an awful run and a mediocre score. When the announcer said "85" I felt all the uselessness of my effort.

## Gus: One Woman's Champion

*Looking back to Gus's First Big Trial Win . . .
and Its Aftermath*

I thought back to the time when Gus was younger, before I ever took him to a Nationals, back to the first year I would even earn enough points to qualify him for Nationals. I had recently moved him up to the Open class. His tension had not yet begun to manifest itself, and he worked easily and naturally for me. He had begun to mature, and that summer, seemingly out of the blue, we won our first major trial, one of the biggest in the west. It marked the moment when I first began to raise the bar on my expectations for his trialing success, and my own.

A top east coast handler, originally Scottish, was the judge, and I had complete confidence in him. The trial was held at a dairy farm in Washington state, a beautiful venue, festive and green, with fine old trees dotting the landscape. The trial host always provided an enormous white canopy, under which handlers and many local spectators gathered to watch the runs; an excellent announcer, who knows most of the dogs, presided over the loud speaker; and full scores were posted almost immediately, with constant revisions to the leader board, which lent excitement.

I was not a very experienced handler and did not yet think of preparing strategies for my run. I was often influenced by those who ran just before me, no matter their strategy or success. As it happened, the handler running just before me was known for running her dogs very slowly, and I watched her carefully. I saw how easily her dog made panels, with plenty of time to take aim or make a correction. I resolved to run Gus this way and to try to slow things down. Because the tension had not yet manifested itself, running him slowly was still an option. I walked to the post with confidence and sent Gus right. He gave me his beautiful natural cast. His sheep were set at the top of a slow rise about 500 yards away.

Three things stand out for me from this run. First, the steadier pace worked, we made the fetch panel, brought the sheep down and around the post and drove them to the first drive panel with a steady flow. I had him nudge the sheep up to and through the panel, then stopped him. But my timing was off. I stopped him too soon, which made the sheep stop awkwardly just inside the panel. They did not quite clear it. If I flanked him, they might turn just inside and miss the panel, at least five points off. If I walked him up, they might spurt through, but then barrel up the field. I might lose the sheep for good or waste precious time and my dog's energy. What to do? I decided to give him the flank whistle, then a quick lie down, hoping his abrupt move would bump them through the panel, but his half flank would force them to move left rather than back up the field. I blew the flank, then a forceful stop. It worked! They moved just a few feet, cleared the panels with a tight turn, then stopped again. I flanked him wide around, and we were on our way to the cross drive.

Second thing I remember is the close work, the shed and pen. Gus pushed them quietly into the shed ring. As I approached cautiously, they sprang apart, three and two. Without thinking, I called Gus in on the two. "Okay!" On to the pen. I had watched a lot of penning at this trial, including one by a top handler who had published a whole teaching video just on the pen. I had observed how he stood back and asked the dog to bring the sheep as close as he could without causing them to turn on the dog or split and run. I did the same. I waited a beat for them to relax at the pen mouth, then flanked Gus around to hold his side. As he moved around them, so did I, until I was directly behind them. Then I stood tall and walked the sheep into the pen. As the gate closed, cheers erupted. I let Gus go to the large trough behind the post and, as I walked off the course, the announcer gave my score: 91. It was a full 10 points higher than any score so far. I was delirious and doffed my hat, an absurdly wrong, male gesture, but I had no other model, and hoped to appear modest, not swooning.

The third thing I resolved was to have the mental discipline to do well again the second day. *I would not be a flash in the pan!* I would deserve this win. Friends started joking they would have to take lessons from me now, and one told me he admired my decision at the drive away panel. Another friend, unaccustomed to seeing so much success come from a middling handler, repeated in a puzzled tone, "But Gus isn't that good a dog, is he?" He expected me to agree! Yet another asked me to make sense of why his dog wouldn't come through on the shed. Not used to my new celebrity, I hazarded that the sheep were squirrelly and touchy, and the dog was afraid of losing them. Only then did it dawn on me that most people had felt the sheep were hard to handle, yet Gus had worked them as if they were a farm flock, had exhibited no tension, but had simply done what I asked. I started to see what a big deal this win was. Next day, I came in second, just behind one of the top handlers in America, placing well as

I had resolved. Someone remarked to me some months later that Gus "put me on the map."

I had made plans to go to the UK with a friend for a few weeks shortly after this trial to visit a famous handler there. I took Gus with me, buoyed by my win at this big trial. But a difficulty occurred. Just as we were starting to have extraordinary success, what seemed like a fatal flaw in Gus emerged. The small flock of blackface ewes that we worked on the hills there became heavier and slower each day, and as they did, Gus found it harder and harder to move them. And when he tried, he moved in an exaggerated wing-wang serpentine, a flank left, then right, a crazed mini-gather. He became frantic.

The trainer quickly yelled, "Stop him! Don't let him do that." His opinion? Gus was weak and must have had a traumatic experience when young to work as frantically and ineffectually as that. This was a dog you would not want in your kennel. The rejection was severe. I was devastated, and he offered no means of help. I was afraid there might be none. What had been an exhilarating victory now turned to a crushing disappointment as I painfully contemplated my dog's fatal flaw, that despite his successes, he was a "weak piece of ****."

I came back to the US reeling from this experience and needing to get to the bottom of this behavior. Was Gus weak and useless, was his eye too strong, what was the diagnosis and what was the cure for this problem? I had no one to turn to. I didn't have a strong mentor at the time who could guide me. I noticed a clinic being given nearby by a top handler who had won the US Nationals several times. I decided to make the pilgrimage to see him and put the problem to him. How could Gus take first and second place at one of the hardest trials in the west, then look so weak on heavy blackfaces? I laid this out for him in a spirit of anxious sorrow. He asked me to first gather, then drive the sheep waiting for us in the ring. These were light Cheviot lambs, and Gus had no trouble moving them. Indeed, I had to slow him down so that they would walk, not scurry about. Then he asked me to single one off, and have Gus hold it against the fence.

We shed off a single ewe, and Gus walked her carefully to the fence. When she felt the fence behind her, she began to move sideways to try to escape. I stood back and watched as Gus flanked out in a gentle arc, caught her a few yards down the fence line, then changed direction and repeated the same pattern as she tried to go the opposite way. This dance went back and forth, the ewe trying to run either way to escape, Gus flanking out and catching her a few yards away. He worked like a cutting horse, never diving in to grip, just holding her steadily and moving his head to stay face to face with her. Each arc she made was smaller than the last. Finally, she saw she could not escape either side and stopped. He had worked her to a standstill.

The clinician said there was no sign of weakness in Gus; bossing a single sheep is one of the hardest things to do. "And," he said, "that was as nice as I've ever seen that done. Not nicer, mind you, but as nice as I've ever seen that done." I knew this handler to be hard on himself and others. Coming from him, those words were high praise indeed. It wasn't until some weeks later, when the setout fellow, who had watched our lesson, called asking to breed to Gus, that I learned that the clinician had liked Gus so much he would have tried to buy him had Gus been a year younger.

In explaining Gus's behavior with the blackfaces, the clinician said that many good dogs meet a few sheep in their trial careers that they cannot shift. It happens to the best of handlers, and he named a top handler who had experienced the same misery as I. But, he said, those experiences are few, and the skills the dog has are considerable and won't stop him from winning most trials. Almost every dog will meet some sheep he can't move, but that won't stop him from being a very good dog.

I tried to take this important perspective into myself, and gradually did so. But for a time, I felt it was a fatal flaw. How could I think my dog was as great as I did, if he could fail me in this way? Was he a goat or a god? I wavered several times a day on this, could not get him into perspective. Could I call him as talented and as beautiful as I thought he was, or did I have "kennel blindness," thinking my dog was the best because he was mine. I desperately needed to understand this. Was Gus a coward and a weakling? Or conversely, as so many people said, was he "a lot of dog?" I could not answer this question. I would have more years of doubt about his fundamental soundness before I realized that Gus had understood this problem, too, and learned on his own to fix it. But about this, more later.

The UK trainer had already disciplined him for gripping when he couldn't move his sheep. I decided to replace the grip with a "stand." I would ask Gus to walk up as close to the sheep as I dared. If the sheep still didn't turn, I would ask him to "stand." This would replace the frantic gathering motion. Ideally after a few seconds of this, the sheep would back up or turn and melt back into its pack. I tried this fix in the shed ring at a Christmas trial a few months later: on my command of "Stand there!" Gus stood almost nose to nose with a ewe who wanted to leave the shed ring. After a few long seconds, she turned and rejoined the others. He had bossed her without a grip or a flank, had held his ground. As a fix, it would have to suffice until I understood him better.

## *Gus's Maturity and Development of His Talent*

Gus, at seven, has gained strength and maturity. He was always a confident dog, but he has matured. Meanwhile, my current trainer has myriad exercises for all kinds of bad habits and weaknesses, including his tendency to get excited and over-flank. In keeping with her instructions, I have frequently worked Gus on a single sheep. The benefit is that the dog must pay complete attention and watch his sheep very carefully as he brings her to you. If the dog slides off the pressure and over-flanks for even a second, the sheep will escape.

I did not realize what effect this work with a single sheep in a small arena would have on a 500-yard gather with a packet of five. But I found out at a nearby California trial. One of the biggest difficulties of this trial was the fetch. As the dog approached his sheep at the top, the sheep would bolt either left or right, and he would spend half of the fetch trying to get them back online. Gus's lift and fetch surprised me: it was dead even and so straight, I gasped. Five heads lined up and came straight forward. That had to be a full points outrun and lift. Now, I thought, the crazy zigzag would begin. It did not.

Gus looked at the packet of five just the way he looked at a single, his body curving slightly to my left to prevent their breaking that way. He scanned each head, moving forward, then slightly to the side, his head doing a slight serpentine all by itself, then moving in a half flank designed to suggest they could move, he would allow it, but only if they moved forward. His tiny gesture invited them to escape, then he closed back in on the pressure, sealing the flank so that forward was the only escape route. They neared the fetch panel. I thought I should step in, start whistling to manage the panel. When I asked for a slight flank to my right, I saw the sheep immediately gather speed and move left. Only then did I realize how forcefully he was holding the pressure and how much better he was at reading it than I. I called out, "Sorry, you're right" and let him continue, only blowing occasional steadies to remind him to take time.

As they neared the post, I became elated. This was an almost flawless gather. We had a shot at a good placement. His pace on the drive was excellent, fast enough to keep a constant flow, but slow enough for precision. With our slower pace, I had time to scan the line to the cross-drive panel. We adjusted with a slight flank to push them behind the panels. These sheep had to be "pulled through" the cross-drive panel from behind. Straight through the middle! At the shed I rotated side to side to stop their forward movement and gain control. I induced two to turn around and walk away and pressured a third to join them. She obliged. I quickly called Gus through. "Good," called the judge. I looked at my watch: almost four minutes out of ten remaining for the pen. If I could get it, I thought we could win.

I knew the pen would be trouble when Gus could not get the sheep close enough to the mouth for me to sidle around. They fought him, lined up against him, stamped at him, and swung their heads. I was behind them and could see nothing of what Gus was up against. I asked for a stand, but they did not melt back. I asked him to flank, stepping forward myself to try to move the sheep. One swung its head at him, and he snapped the air in front of its face. I growled to warn him off a grip. Several times the sheep got close, he came around, and the sheep retreated from the mouth again. We gradually narrowed this arc until they were finally in the mouth. I probably should have waited and settled them here, but I hoped to stand tall and walk them in. Four went in, the fifth ducked through my rope and escaped. I looked at my watch. Six seconds left. We stood still for six seconds and let the judge call time.

Later, I looked at my score: 87. With ten off for the pen not made, I had lost only three points from the rest of the run. As close to perfection as it gets. Watching the rest of the runs and hoping my score would hold was nerve wracking. One almost perfect run with a pen got a 90. I left shortly thereafter and had a long ride home wondering if our second place would hold. Later that night a friend sent me a picture of the scoreboard. Yes, we came second without a pen. Almost every placing run had done it with some pen points. We had one off the fetch, two off the drive, plus ten for no pen. I was proud of Gus's beautiful steady pressure on the sheep, his slinky suave movements, and his courage at the pen. We had practiced it, and we were like two circus performers who know our routine cold and trust each other at the balancing act.

I am reading a wonderful book by the late handler and trainer Vergil Holland about handling at a competition. He argues that you can teach border collies, as well as other breeds, to perform a series of rote, intricate maneuvers such as are seen in agility, fly ball, or advanced obedience. What you cannot teach, and where sheep work differs from these sports, is the *innovative* step your border collie will take to help you in a new situation, with new sheep and new difficulties. This is the border collie intellect at work, or perhaps this is another way of saying some border collies have such keen intelligence and understanding of the task at hand that they instinctively perform a maneuver that could never have been taught, that you could not have dreamed your dog would do, but once done, you see how much he was telling you about the sheep, how his understanding of the task and his sheep allowed you to achieve the desired result.

Tony McCallum, noted stockman and dog handler, describes this same talent for innovation, but he uses different words to name it. He calls it magic. Responding to someone who maintains there is no magic in sheepdog training, just repetition of exercises, he says:

> No, to be sure there is a little magic. No amount of hard work, practice, repetition will hit the heights of that moment of magic. When you are in a position of dire straits, on the side of a mountain, you know for sure perhaps days of work

are about to come undone, wild stock you have battled days to capture, are about to scream down a gorge and escape. You know nothing that you and your dog have done, practiced, rehearsed or memorized is going to stop it. Then in a heartbeat, your dog does something that should not even have worked, something it should not have been physically even possible for him to do. He does it because of a work ethic deep inside him, and because of the bond you have built in those years of hard work, but this goes beyond training and practice, and the day you are part of it, you will feel the Magic. And I can tell you, if you pay very close attention when it is all done, I swear to you, the dog will give you a look and a barely noticeable wink, as he follows those stock as if nothing happened.

This is the heart of the matter, the things your dog does for you that you could not have trained for, even thought of. And yet he does it because of a work ethic and a bond with you. This is the feeling, almost eerie, of magic that I have about Gus. I will give a few examples from my own experience.

Some time back, I went to a northern California trial. The sheep there live on that field and are calm with people, nervous only around new dogs. The shed at this trial was especially tricky, as it is the first place the sheep are confined in a small space, squeezed between handler and dog. Many handlers had tried to make a split by asking their dog to flank back and forth, to induce two sheep to go left, two to go right, so that the dog could come through, but it did not work. The sheep as a group simply ran around, in and out of the ring, and could not be settled. Many teams using this method timed out without getting their shed. We tried this for perhaps thirty seconds but had the same trouble as others. I was out of ideas. I flanked Gus around to regroup the sheep, not knowing what to try next.

He surprised me by flanking quite far off his sheep and lying down at a considerable distance from them. I looked at him curiously for long seconds. This was not his usual way, which was to hook around close, lean into his sheep to put pressure on them, and run in once a hole was made. I wondered whether he was ill. Just then I happened to glance at the sheep. They were no longer tense and flighty, with heads carried high and stiff, eyes flashing and tongues nervously licking lips. They had become calm and still, their heads carried in a relaxed position. They seemed attentive, their heads tilted toward me, looking slightly past me in a deferential manner.

A sense of power and confidence washed over me, and I relaxed. They seemed to be inviting me to move them as I wished, I would get no argument from them. I looked back at Gus, this time measuring the distance. I quickly calculated that if I made a quiet hole, not too big, which might cause them to rejoin, I might be able to call Gus in. He normally comes in smoothly and quickly, without upsetting his sheep.

I was taking a chance. If he was too far away and the sheep rejoined before he came through, I would lose 5 of my 10 points before I even got a shed. But if I walked him up first, the sheep would get touchy again. I had tried that, and it didn't work. I decided to try for the shed from that distance. I rotated my body to make the hole, first left, then right, as a great Scottish handler had taught me. The sheep moved apart obediently, without hesitation or resistance. All was calm. I leaned forward, stretched out a hand, called "Gus, this!" and turned on the left two. He propelled himself through the hole, turned on the two. "Good!" shouted the judge. I thought I heard a spectator gasp.

Later, I saw we had zero off our shed. Gus's curious behavior did not come back to me for a couple of days. I was startled when it did. At first all I remembered was the rising panic I felt when I realized I was in a jam at the shed and had no solution to the problem. I felt the panic all over again. Then I replayed what happened next. Gus had flanked far off his sheep, and that had relaxed the sheep enough to achieve the shed. Though I had not understood this at the moment, it was a perfect example of innovation that Gus brought to the task at hand. It was the only way we were going to get that shed with those sheep. What did he know and what was he thinking? Did he reason that out?

Vergil goes on to say that by the time the dog has brought his sheep into the shed ring, he knows his sheep far better than his handler does. The dog has met them at the top of the field and has taken them all around the course, whereas I, stepping into the shed ring, am only feeling my sheep for the first time. This knowledge set the stage for Gus's specific innovation. Can one ask whether a dog "consciously" thinks of kicking himself out, so that his handler can make a hole and get the shed? Or is it just a highly refined instinct that makes the dog, without thinking, cast himself out in order to calm his sheep? Is this what one would call talent in a working border collie? To me, it is. To me this phenomenon is at the very heart of the mystery and the magic of the border collie's immense talent, of Gus's immense talent.

One final important lesson in my understanding of Gus's abilities came entirely from him and remained for a long time unremarked by me. My trainer recently commented that many excellent UK dogs imported to the western US to compete on our range ewes end up disappointing their new owners. They often have strong eye, which they use to control their sheep. The strong eye is perceived as the threat of a predator by our range sheep, slows them down and prevents their moving around the course easily, creating standoffs and grips. Puzzled, I pointed out that Gus has quite a bit of eye, yet as a mature dog has had no problem moving sheep. My trainer responded, "Gus has taught himself how to move range ewes" by averting his strong eye when he needed to. This utterly astonished me until I remembered a day when I was working Gus on some stroppy ewes.

There were 100 ewes in a big field; we had shed off ten and were taking them to the other end of the field. The draw back to the 90 is very strong, but Gus knew to be on guard and not let the ten escape. One stroppy ewe kept giving him trouble, breaking off from the group and trying to run back. Finally, she turned and faced him, while the others marched ahead. He blocked her path by standing firmly in front of her as I had taught him, but I noticed he looked first to her left, then to her right, *averting his gaze and never locking eyes with her.* At the same time he moved his body slightly side to side as if to gather her up. I could see he was worried that he would lose the others while he was dealing with her. The gathering motion he made with his body while averting his gaze convinced her she could not get past him. She turned and rejoined the group. He had avoided a confrontation, handled her and managed to keep the group together. This is why, since that traumatic moment when Gus was unable to move the blackfaces, *he never again got stuck while moving sheep*. But I would not have realized that he had taught himself to do that if not for my trainer's comment. I marvel at it still.

# Chapter 2: Trialing in the UK

We would go to England. My husband came into the bedroom, sat me down in our two comfy chairs, and spoke of his desire to spend his sabbatical doing research at Cambridge University. Between his sabbatical and the summer months, we could spend more than five months there. I breathed deeply, contemplating what it could mean for Gus and me. It was a great step into the unknown and back to the heartland of sheepdogs, sheep, and trialing. It was the home of the greatest of the "old testament" names—J. R. Thomas's Craig and Don, Bobby Dalziel's Wisp and Dryden Joe, Johnny Wilson's Spot—to name just a few of the greatest dogs, most Supreme champions, some multiple times. The Supreme Champion, or simply "Supreme," is the dog-handler team that has won the International, the annual competition among the top fifteen handlers from each of the four nations—England, Ireland, Scotland and Wales. These ancient dogs, no longer living, live on in the pedigrees of many current champions. There were families of shepherds and farmers who had bred great dogs for generations. I wanted to penetrate to the heart of this mysterious activity and to the mystery of Gus's tension. I was silent for several long seconds, contemplating the chance to crack this mystery. It would be a lot of work, to find the right teacher, gain access to sheep and a field to practice on, make friends, learn how to drive on the "wrong" side of the road, and decide which trials to go to.

I resolved I would campaign Gus, show him to top handlers, find out once and for all whether he had the talent I saw, or whether I was "kennel-blind," committing the grievous error of believing fervently in your dog just because he is yours and you love him, not recognizing greater talent when you see it. Committing the error of having self-regard blind you to real learning and understanding, without which you could never advance, even with the dogs you had. I returned to the moment, smiled and said, "Yes, oh yes! What a wonderful adventure it will be!"

He quickly told me of his plan that we should live outside of Cambridge and find a small village where I could make training arrangements. I smiled at his generosity in thinking so much on my behalf. It spoke to his own excitement about his prospects for widening his horizons, working out complications in the book he was writing, his hopes for inspiration there. That defined both of our pilgrimages, to penetrate deeper into the respective mysteries we had created for ourselves.

## First Trials in the UK

We settled into a comfortable, fully furnished, rather large house on the high street of a village outside Cambridge with Gus and Zac. We quickly bought a ten-year old diesel station wagon—a tank—of which I would be the main driver. I took a few driving lessons from the driver who met our plane at Heathrow, studied videos explaining the rules of roundabouts and memorized road signs. I had worked Gus steadily before we left, knowing his obedience might quickly deteriorate if he was not drilled thoroughly while I still had sheep to work on. I wanted to trial him before that happened. To that end, I signed up for our first trial within a week of arriving in the UK.

The trial was not far from Cambridge. My husband came with me. He was protective of me, not yet confident of my driving skills. I was grateful. Without being able to drive, I was almost helpless, as there were few trials in the immediate area. I needed to drive to get to meet people, see how good stockmen handled their dogs, and learn about the tricks of each course. This trial was, as was often the case, on the grounds of an important country manor. These usually had their own flocks. That meant that, as opposed to those in the US, the sheep were comfortable in their environment, knew the terrain, did not feel a strong need to escape to the exhaust pen, and so could be worked more neutrally. Also, unlike the US, where you either ran a farm flock that might have seen many trials, or had unbroke range ewes who had rarely seen dogs, these sheep knew dogs, but still had to be bossed to be moved.

At the trial I fell in with a couple of handlers who knew a handler I knew from back in the US. They clearly respected him a lot and talked freely with me as though I were an old friend. They had first names I had never heard before, like Eammon and Huw. They were very witty, told stories and gave a lot of what, in the UK, was called "good craic" as various handlers came to the post. I knew from my time at US trials that there are always many sides to a story that we do not know, so I said nothing, but found it hard to contain myself, as their dry wit was very amusing.

The afternoon wore on, and I was up. I had studied the runs and thought I understood the course well enough. In truth it was not a difficult course, but the sheep were touchier than I realized. I had not noticed how gingerly the best handlers worked their dogs, holding them quite far back. In any case, that would have been next to impossible with Gus. The English called him "a bit full on." This could mean anything from what Americans approvingly called "plenty of forward" to pushing them down your throat on the fetch. I had worked on this at home and hoped the results of my training would be felt today. Gus gave me his typical flawless outrun and brought them a bit fast, coming nicely through the fetch gates. Drive lines were a bit wobbly due to his pushiness, but we made the panels. We typically achieved a smooth and quick shed, so I took the first hole presented and called him through. That started a ping pong effect, and the two he was supposed to hold split off and zoomed away in two different directions. It was like taking two singles at once. Gus worked independently, flanking and gathering, got them back under control and drove them away. We penned carefully and without incident.

I rejoined the others and said not a word about my run. After the ribbing other handlers had received, I feared to raise any point or draw attention to it. Shortly thereafter I ran into a Facebook friend and introduced myself. We talked avidly for several minutes. She ended with, "I didn't see your run, but it must have been good because [my new buddies] are saying they really like your dog." I exhaled deeply and relaxed. That was so important to know, that they did not think me a naïve, kennel blind American, but rather someone who could deliver a good run and not parade it. I went back and sat down with them and enjoyed the rest of the afternoon.

I ran into the two at several more trials and enjoyed them. Months later, I was at a difficult trial with a double gather on the last day, where one of the fellows was running a dog. We stood together, and he talked in his usual dry manner. I had finally had the presence of mind to sit and watch his qualifying run and his double gather run. I thought both were excellent, but his scores seemed not to reflect the control and refinement he showed. I pushed myself to mention it, worried I would strike the wrong note and intrude. At first he was diffident and did not betray any feeling about his scores. Finally, he relented, and accepted my protestations. There was a story there, but he was not going to tell me what it was. But he appreciated my comments, was touched. I could tell that.

I referred to his run being so much better than my own, and how wrong it was that our scores were separated by only a few points. He responded, "Yes, I saw your mistakes, but that dog has never let you down, never." I stopped in my tracks at these words. On the one hand, I was not sure exactly what that meant. He had only seen Gus a few times. On the other hand, it sounded exactly right. Gus never had. And it was immensely consoling, as if he had gotten the genius of the dog right, had sensed his absolute passion to do whatever he was asked, whatever it took to get it done. I'll never know whether he merely handed out a commonly heard compliment or perceived the utter commitment of the dog. But he had got it right. In the end I was glad

I had spoken to him. Something good had transpired between us.

We had been in the UK three weeks or so, and I still had no place to train. Knowing Gus, I feared the discipline I had instilled in him before we left would dissipate quickly without a place to train and reinforce obedience every day. I had already beseeched a local contact I had made on Facebook, only to be resoundingly, even coldly rejected. It seemed that unless I took lessons from this person, no arrangement, even a paying one, was possible. I asked, and asked others to ask. The answer was consistently and unapologetically, "No."

In the meantime, the dogs had to be kept in shape. We accomplished this in a makeshift manner. In addition to an hour's daily walk, which is just about nothing to a border collie, my husband and I took them out to the local park every evening shortly before dusk. I had prepared small cubes of cheese. They always came willingly to me, but would not willingly leave me, so my husband had to bait the trap with cheese. We walked to the small park nearby, then separated. He took the dogs to one end, I walked to the other end. I blew their recall whistle on sheep and called their names. They galloped toward me, flat out, circled me, and stopped. I waved my arm to my husband. They consented to leave me and toddle back to him, but only after I made a low, vibrating *zzz-zzz* sound that always made them want to run. I could see him rewarding them with the small cubes of cheese at the top of the field. We did this back and forth six to seven times, which might correspond to the energy expended on a single outrun, leashed them, and returned to the house. I knew it could never substitute for regular sheep work.

I voiced my concern to our Cambridge friends, to whom the sheep world was utterly remote, and Angela got an idea. Her village had its own Facebook page. She posted on it that she had a friend looking for sheep to work, and could walkers who walked the hills report back on the whereabouts of any sheep they encountered? I got two responses on the community page. The first was from a couple of walkers who encountered a local farmer who, they said, constantly swore at his dog for not penning the sheep competently, leaving some and making a bad job of it. They asked other walkers on the Facebook page whether anyone knew the identity of the "Angry Farmer" as they referred to him. Others chimed in with derisive comments on the farmer's mismanagement. Two days later, another comment appeared, from "the Wife of the Angry Farmer." She lambasted the walkers for leaving their dogs to run loose, as they ran about out of control, pushing the sheep out of the pen that the farmer's dog had indeed carefully penned. I apologized on the walkers' behalf, explaining most have no idea how difficult and touchy sheep can be nor their dogs' effect on them. That apology, however, was not sufficient to gain me a response or access to that farmer's sheep.

My second response was from a lone walker, who walked on one of the hills surrounding Cambridge. She saw a large flock and a sign with a telephone number on it regarding the sheep. I assumed this was the flock belonging to some great house, and I would be coldly and politely rebuffed by a patrician voice. I waited two days to muster the courage to call it. A friendly, hearty voice answered. I haltingly began what suddenly struck me as a preposterous request for access to his sheep and waited for the rejection. He paused and said, "How many sheep do you need?" I answered with as many as I dared, "Ten?" He said that would be all right, and we should probably meet. We made a date for the following day, and I turned up with my dogs at his father's farm, named The Rectory, a sweet house about five miles from our village with a garden and many stone outbuildings, surrounded by a whitewashed plaster fence. Many tractors and other farm equipment were parked in the yard. I later learned that he was one of the largest sheep farmers in Cambridgeshire. I met his son, a soft-spoken, alert, sensible fellow in his early 20's, and his father, a twinkly, somewhat stooped 70-year old.

He spoke of his young dog, who was proving hard to start. After hearing that two or three times, I hesitantly asked whether he would like me to have a go at training him. He thought I would never ask. Then he asked again, "How many sheep do you need?" I hazarded "twenty-five?" He said "done!" showed me a lovely green, treed field behind the house, and said I could come and go as I pleased, and work whenever I wanted. I tried to express the gratitude I felt, but as with so many I encountered in the UK, this was a hard emotion to negotiate. He cut me short, smiled and shook hands, and it was done. I could hardly believe my good fortune.

Thanks to him, I could start training in earnest. I had by now been to several local trials and was beginning to notice some of the differences between US and UK trials. In the UK, there was always something that created a difficulty that did not seem like much until you had to manage it. For one thing, UK setout people barely held the sheep at the top. They nudged them out of the pen and in the general direction of the setout spot. They rarely held them with hay, as most fields were replete with thick grass, which was much more tempting to sheep than hay. I saw people start to send their dogs well before the sheep arrived at the setout spot. They seemed to try to time their dog's arrival at the top to the moment when the sheep arrived there on their own. I wondered how the lift could be judged, but I was still too busy trying to figure out the strategy for when to send one's dog. The sheep in this part of the country did not seem very hard to move, in fact, were rather light.

This was not the best for Gus, who was "full on" in the extreme. His tension level when working unfamiliar sheep had grown as he had aged, and I had trouble controlling his pace. I had to hold him back and lie him down several times on the fetch, if I could, to maintain correct distance. This was seen as a fault in the UK, while a smooth, seamless, constant pace executed with finesse and fine footwork was rewarded. I watched as one lean, dark collie in particular paced so well in turning the post that he repeatedly crossed one front and one back leg over the other as he made the almost 360-degree turn, like a ballet step. His pace was a steady, sensitive walk which did not need to be quickened or slowed to keep the sheep at a steady slow trot. I knew Gus could set his paws elegantly like this, but for him the job of moving sheep far outranked fine footwork. With such light sheep, we had to move haltingly around the course. Our starts and stops perturbed the sheep enough that the line was broken up with just that bit of weaving by the sheep that generally kept us out of the points.

Another difference was the number of "distractions" on the field. In this part of the UK, trials were sometimes run on heavily treed fields. The course might be designed so that if your dog lifted his sheep sideways instead of straight toward you, they might vanish behind a tree. The post, where the handler must stand for most of the run, might be right next to another tree, with low hanging branches. If the dog pushed the sheep off the fetch line, you might have to get down on your hands and knees to see your dog and manage your fetch. I found these conditions broke my concentration and hurt my runs. This was much more about me, my age, my poor eyesight, and my enormous physical clumsiness than it was about my dog.

Yet another variant might be a small hillock that was chosen for the set out of the sheep. With the loose holding, if your dog did not arrive at the post early enough (say, because the previous handler did not clear his sheep away in time), by the time you got to the post, the sheep had disappeared behind the hillock and were now invisible. Your dog had no opportunity to spot his sheep before beginning his outrun. This was known as a blind outrun, was one of the more difficult trialing challenges, and could end with the dog retiring without ever finding his sheep.

One of the first trials I went to in England had a particularly difficult version of this challenge. There was a longish outrun, about 400 yards up a slow grade. The sheep were set just at the brow of the hill. The handler could see the sheep's heads as long as they didn't bolt back; the dog, much lower to the ground, could not see them at all. Everyone had his dog watch earlier runs, so they could see what direction the sheep came from. There was a second difficulty if you sent right. Most did, because the terrain on the right enabled the dogs to see their sheep sooner than sending left, which was almost entirely blind. But on the right, there was a quirk in the terrain: the low grass ended near the top of the hill and was replaced by taller grass. The taller grass was seen by the dogs as a boundary and caused many dogs to turn in too soon. As a result, they approached the sheep sideways, if not from below, and a frantic chase ensued, usually resulting in the sheep bounding back to the setout pen and the team retiring. I had the benefit of an acquaintance who described this to me and cautioned me to watch carefully in case Gus turned in early.

I was ready for it. When our turn came, I stared at the sheep on the brow of the hill. Gus always looked where I was looking. I took a small step straight forward, to show him the central axis of his outrun, and said "away." He made a beautiful cast out to the right. Just before he reached the top of the grade, I saw him take one step in rather than continuing his arc. I blew a stop, then a turnback whistle. He kicked out immediately, right through the tall grass to the fence, and vanished over the hill.

Then I saw a sheep's head or two but could see nothing else. Long seconds passed, and the packet still did not come down. I could not help him as I could see nothing. I knew the group had split, and he was trying to round them up. Finally, I saw them break over the brow, not at the lift spot, but much farther to the left. It had clearly been messy. Well, that was forgotten as I blew a hard steady and reproved him with a sharp "Gus!" He slowed, the packet straightened out, and they sidled down the hill in a stately minuet, delicately moving on a slight oblique line to arrive at the fetch panel without making obvious adjustments. As they slid through the fetch panels, I relaxed and managed him gently down to the handler's post. They came straight on and around the post.

As I turned to follow them around the post, I was startled to see that the judge had come out of the judging box and was standing behind me. He disqualified me with a low "thank you" and explained the setout had radioed from the top that Gus had gripped. I was shocked and apologetic. One cannot treat sheep this way. But of course, I could neither see nor control anything at the top. I cleared my sheep off and left. Gus had been a frequent gripper at the lift when young but had not done that for a long time. I thought it was possible he had instead bunted a sheep with his mouth closed. He has a sort of slap with his closed muzzle that he used to discipline an unruly sheep, which I had seen him use at times. Not many dogs have this move, so it was understandable that this was either mistaken for a grip, or was still considered unacceptable, as it involved the dog touching the sheep. I will never know. I am still to this day smarting from this DQ. It was one of my first trials in the UK, and I was hypersensitive to how he would be regarded. I wanted no identification with "wild west" behavior.

Back in East Anglia, there was an elaborate two-day trial with three fields, where each dog ran on two of the three fields on day one. Day two was a double gather reserved for the day's top five finalists from each of the three fields. I won't dwell on the first field we ran on except to say that instead of proper panels, thin metal gates were used. It was an overcast day, and in the somber morning light, when we ran, these simply vanished. I occasionally caught a glimpse of the panels and tried to associate them with a nearby tree, but then they vanished again. To me it seemed a field with no obstacles at all. I was unhappy about it but could do nothing except take my turn with inevitably bad results.

Once I had recovered myself, I went down to visit the second field, hoping to watch several runs before ours. As I arrived, a tremendous wind blew up. Later I learned these were gale force winds of 50 MPH. I examined the field, which appeared slightly convex, so that it was hard to see the sheep clearly at their set out point from the post. Most handlers sent right. This seemed suboptimal, as the field sloped slightly down on the right side, which might impede the dogs seeing their sheep. The terrain was also open on the right, with a number of trees; dogs might go out too wide, lose their bearings, and never find their sheep. Indeed, while I watched, several teams did just that. I was not too concerned, because Gus always sees his sheep. With this advantage, I approached the post confidently. I decided to send him left. It was his second run of the morning, and I did not want him getting tired from an overly wide outrun. There were large rocks and the beginnings of a hill on the left, which might act as a boundary and keep him in as I wanted.

By this time the wind was an assault on the body, and it was raining quite hard. I had three hats on, a baseball cap against the glare, a beanie against the wind, and the hood of my slicker against the rain. Thus outfitted, it was almost impossible to turn my head. Gus stood next to me at the post, crouching, and together we silently regarded a spot about 700 yards away, where I could see a vague blur which I took to be the sheep. I took a small step straight forward and said "come bye" in a low tone.

He ran out with purpose. I followed him around, only losing sight of him for an instant or two in the tall grass or behind a rock. There was no need to whistle or redirect him; he went out perfectly. In any case the wind was coming straight at me from his direction; he could not have heard me. Even though it was probably useless, I blew him down on the top, then simply had to leave it to him, as I could not yell "steady" loudly enough for him to hear. The wind hit me in the throat, and all guidance was useless. He brought them reasonably straight, if a bit too fast. The drive I hardly remember at all, except that I had a panicky feeling that even at close range he could hardly hear me over the din of the storm. The run seemed doomed. Still, with Gus's speed, we completed the drive and still had good time for the shed and pen. These were two of our strong suits, especially the shed. He always knew which two I wanted and came in like a shot. So it was here. At the pen the sheep were uneasy and unsettled due to the high wind. We went at it methodically, a bit of pressure from his side, then my side, then his side again. As he sidled around toward the edge of the pen, so did I, bringing the gate around to cut off their exit. A bit more pressure, and we had them in.

I left the trial full of unexpressed emotion. I desperately wanted to qualify for the double gather final the next day. But the blustery weather conditions had made that almost impossible. I had watched some runs that came after mine. The wind had died down, a bit of sun came out, and it seemed like a different trial. The sheep were obliging, handlers could whistle gently to their canine teammate without fear of having their commands swallowed by the wind, and peace settled over the field. I saw one or two runs that were clearly better than mine and felt helpless with my bad luck at running in the wind. I mourned that Gus's greatness would continue undiscovered, uncelebrated yet again. As hard as I could try, as smart as I tried to be about my handling, our time had not yet come. I tried to wait around for scores, but they had stopped updating them. I went home and brooded with frustration.

Toward late afternoon, I combed the sheepdog society website to see who had qualified. Shocked and pleased, I saw my name! I had come in fifth on the second field. I was happy and excited. I put it all down to Gus, who had gone out so beautifully on the left. If he could not see them at my feet, he cast out as he ran down the field until he could. Everything else about our run had been mediocre, swallowed by the wind, but no one could take his beautiful gather away from him. Suddenly everything was different. Nature and luck were not conspiring against us! We would live to fight another day!

The next day I turned up a few minutes before the start. They never had handlers' meetings in the UK; the courses were assumed to be self-explanatory. And no one ever inquired about the time allowed for each run; there was usually enough time if proper progress occurred. This was to be a double lift, called a "double gather" in the UK (the dog gathers first one set of ten sheep, then, on the "look back!" command, he turns back for a second group of ten, which he cannot see until he has committed to turn back and run out for the second group). The course was set on a field I had not seen before. I stared at the field without seeing a single obstacle, they were placed that far away. As I scanned the horizon, the president of the society came up to me and kindly volunteered to explain the course to me. He prefaced his remarks by saying, "If you think some double gathers are harder than others, you should know that this host is known for designing devilishly difficult courses, much harder than most, and this course is no exception." He advised me not to feel bad if my dog were unable to navigate the entrance into the upper field, where the sheep were set, and the exit through a different set of gates he would have to use to bring his sheep down. I could hardly grasp what he was saying and couldn't see any openings at all. I knew the challenge would be very great. I still did not understand the course at all.

The course was set on three contiguous fields that rose in a steady, even upslope about 700 yards, fenced on all sides. I was told, but could not really make out, that there was a wide and deep creek separating the second field from the third, with high grass and bracken growing along it that obscured a handler's view of his dog. The dog needed to make his way out the first field through a gate into the second field, run to the top, then cross the creek, using a narrow plank laid over it, into the third field, always ascending.

Once emerging from the bracken, he had to continue *straight up* a steeper upslope another 100 yards to the top of that field to find his first set of sheep. It was still a blind outrun even after he crossed into the third field! Only dogs like Gus, who had the natural instinct to cast out when they could not see their sheep, would continue straight up rather than crossing over in front of their sheep. What happened after that I would not be sure of until the first team to get that far showed me where to bring the sheep down. The dog needs to stop at about two o'clock to bring the sheep slantwise across the field to a *different* bridge that led to the lower part of the field and then down to a point about 100 yards above the handler's post. The dog would drop the first set of sheep here and then turn back to the left for the second gather.

I watched the runs with concentration and excitement, straining to see where the bridge was. The society president was up. I watched him closely. He stood with his dog about 20 yards behind the post he would eventually man and appeared to try to show his dog where the first set of sheep was located. He stood at an angle and watched the spot fixedly. Once the sheep were set, he walked with his dog at that angle to the post, then turned sideways to the field, faced his dog, who stood beside him, did a sort of plie akin to a conductor giving the upbeat, stretched out his hand to the right, took a full step sideways and sent him with a low "Away." The dog understood the body language and moved straight sideways until he reached the fence.

It was only then I realized that the gate to the second field was right at the fence line. Sending the dog sideways to the fence enabled the dog to easily locate the opening to the next field. He had done something interesting in his communication with his dog. Away from the post, he showed him where the sheep were, his ultimate destination; at the post, he showed him the route he had to take to get there. I had never encountered anything like this indirection before. At US trials, there were rarely any impediments to the dog's doing a "natural," pear shaped outrun; no special instructions were needed.

I was full of admiration for the subtlety of these instructions and his dog's comprehension. He went out the gate, up the second field and bam! right over the plank into the third field. But as soon as he emerged from the bridge, he turned in, casting narrowly across the field *below* his sheep. Because of the bracken, the handler could not see the dog until it was too late to redirect him to cast out and up. He had crossed the imaginary line between the sheep and the post and would retire. Several other dogs retired, most not finding their first set of sheep, some not even finding their way into the second field. Because they could not see their sheep, some youngsters did only a halfhearted outrun, circled the lower field uncertainly and came back. So far, I had seen only one dog bring his sheep down, after many redirects. He refused to take the redirect to gather his second set, and so retired. I knew Gus had an excellent, willing turnback; if we could bring the first set down, he would go out without hesitation for his second set.

We were up! I understood the first gather well by now and decided to try the same method with Gus, though we had never done this before. I stood off from the post and gazed in the direction of the first set, my chest facing them, saying nothing. I could see Gus was looking where I looked. That was his way. We stood together without moving, then walked together on an oblique line to the post. Gus's outrun would be a continuation of that line. I turned to him, beckoned sideways to the fence, bent my knees slightly, and sent him. He ran to the fence with purpose, then turned and started up the field. After that, I could see nothing. He was hugging the fence, where the grass was tall. I had no idea how long it would take to get to the bridge and so was helpless to direct him. I stood in anxious silence. Suddenly I saw him. He had shot over the narrow bridge and darted into view on the upper field. Instead of turning in here, as some dogs had, he cast out to the fence, continued straight up the fence line, then disappeared again behind tall grass just as he reached his sheep.

He was the only dog so far to reach his first packet with no redirects! This was his natural instinct kicking in—to cast out and out until he spotted his sheep. I was elated; his outrun was spectacular, heroic, intrepid. But here was a new problem. Instead of stopping at two o'clock to lift on the correct oblique line toward the center bridge, he ran through my stop whistle to slightly past 12 and began to bring them straight down the way he came. I blew a hasty, belated stop whistle, though I could not see him in the tall grass. He ignored it. I blew another stop and yelled his name. Ignored me again. By now he had them back down to the creek and was vainly trying to push them onto the single plank. But it was too narrow for them; they would not go. I lost sight of dog and sheep momentarily and did not know what to do. Then the course director asked me to recall my dog. She said he was marauding the sheep against the fence and needed to be recalled immediately.

I called him, and after a short while, he reappeared in the lower field. I walked off in shame. Marauding sheep was outside the bounds of good stockmanship. As I was leashing him, a shepherd known for being a good dog man came up to me and said, "That's a good dog you have there!" I stared at him, stunned. I had just fouled out in the most miserable way. He explained, "That dog never gave up. He didn't know the field, didn't know there was another route down. This was the only route he knew to bring you sheep, and he was going to do that. Nothing else mattered to him. That's what I call a good dog." I nodded hesitantly, not sure how to evaluate that comment.

I knew Gus had a strong urge to bring sheep, never left any behind, but I assumed all border collies had that urge, some just more strongly than others. I had heard that some border collies lose their interest in sheep work when they get old. I couldn't picture Gus being one of them. I used to joke that he would bring me sheep until the day he died, perhaps even the day after. I didn't yet appreciate the full significance of that urge.

I went back to talking to a lady whose name I did not know. Suddenly one of the judges came out of the stand, walked over to me and said, "That was the best outrun of the day! We will say nothing of what followed, but—that was the best outrun of the day!" I turned to the lady and said I knew that judge, and he was very nice, came out just to make me feel better, and that I liked him so much! She smiled at me and said, "That's my husband!" I grinned broadly at her and said I would like to come up and visit. She said, "Yes, please do, ask him to take you out and show you his dogs. He'd be delighted to!" Suddenly I felt a bit better. In spite of our "cowboy" behavior, I was going to visit someone I thought could become a real friend.

## *Trialing Farther Afield*

By now I was excited. The difficulties that UK handlers took for granted were beginning to dawn to me. The shortest way to the sheep was not the most direct way: various obstacles had to be negotiated, and a dog that could not think, look and listen on the way out could not prevail. *A dog that could not reason, could not delay gratification, could not store experiences and learn from them, could not prevail.* I knew I had a dog that could do all this and more. A dog that had a built-in highly attuned GPS, could run out 500 yards *behind* the hill that the sheep were set on the front face of and come up over the top, landing right behind them. For the first time I studied the ISDS trials diary for trials all over the UK, not just England, ready to go anywhere to campaign my champion. I looked in Wales and Scotland, toggling between the trial names and a map. Welsh names were difficult to spell, impossible to pronounce. I had to carefully match up the letters to make sure I had the right place name on the map.

The one that jumped out at me was a double gather trial in Wales. Normally the double gather is only offered to those who have qualified in the preceding days; you must win your spot in it. There is even an expression for it. A "last day" dog or a "Sunday" dog is one who is strong enough to move a mob of twenty sheep, not just the five used in the qualifying runs. Gus would come to be called a Sunday dog for his strength, stamina and power. But the trick was qualifying, not always easy for the stronger dogs who moved sheep fast and determinedly. Signing up for a double gather would give me the chance to do two gathers and a shed of marked sheep without having to qualify and risk being eliminated. This double gather trial was called Talgarreg. I found it on the map, emailed my desire to enter, and talked to a kindly man who told me to watch for the signs. It was four and a half hours away. I reflected that this was the same distance as one of the closer California trials that I usually attended. I sometimes drove up, ran my dog, and drove home all in the same day.

I thought about Talgarreg with great anticipation. I knew Gus had a totally reliable turnback, and I was excited about showing it off. Since that was the case, I barely did any preparation, convinced I had this one totally under control. I set out for Wales, my first trip there alone. I had gone over the route the night before and made a list of the major highways I would be taking, just in case I met with a sign I had encountered before near Manchester—"Priorities have changed/Ignore satnav." More than once this sign had filled me with dread, as I had no idea which highway to choose, and had ended up going miles out of my way. This time I was prepared!

All went smoothly until I got within ten miles or so of the trial. Then I lost the route, stared at my satnav while driving, and tried to rely on the general direction. That inattention made me go up on sidewalks more than usual. A car pulled up beside me, and the driver rolled down his window and made a gesture of drinking from a glass. I stared at him, then realized he thought I was drunk. I explained I was lost and asked if he knew where the trial was. He demurred and drove off. As I got closer, I saw another car creeping along, looking from field to field. I realized they were looking for the trial, too. After twenty minutes of guesswork, we saw a very small sign on which "DOG TRIAL" was scribbled with a light red sharpie. A sign from the gods! We eagerly turned in, parked, laughed with one another in relief, and sat down to watch.

The Talgarreg trial was recognized as a challenging course. It was set in a huge field on a long, gradually upward sloping hill with a narrow ravine running the length of the field on the left. It looked to be at least a 600-yard outrun. The field was beautifully green and lush. Cars were parked outside the entry to the field. Most handlers congregated near their cars, if at all, so there was little chance to strike up a conversation. I sat down well behind the handler's post to watch. As with many trials in the UK, there was no set run order. When you were ready to run, you put your name on the course director's list, then were usually up in about five or six runs.

Several things dismayed me right off the bat. This was the first trial I had ever seen where the sheep were set on the identical spot for both outruns. I had never thought of this. Usually the second outrun is set in a wide V formation from the first, and dogs generally expect that. I did not know whether Gus would consent to go back to exactly the same spot for the second gather as for the first, the difference being that he had to run out to the right for the second outrun instead of left. The second thing I noticed was that *both* outruns were blind. The first outrun was in itself quite challenging. To cast correctly to the left, the dog had to descend almost immediately into the ravine. In the middle of the ravine there was a fence that bisected it, with a small open gate through to the top. He *had* to come that way or he could not get to the top of the field. After watching several runs, I thought I understood the course well enough to enter my name into the run order.

Gus ran out, down into the ravine and through the gate with no hesitation. I was surprised how easily he found it. He came up out of the ravine on his own, saw the sheep and cast out nicely. He brought the sheep down quietly, got them through an opening in an abandoned fence at the bottom of the field that I hadn't paid much attention to, and to the cone, which was the drop off point for the first set. After this he would turn back for his second set.

I flanked him to the right, asked for a lie down, and blew my turnback whistle. He turned immediately, took a few steps and found his way blocked by the abandoned fencing. The importance of this fence now began to dawn on me. I hadn't studied its openings, didn't see there was one at the far right that I should have redirected him to, so blew him to the left, where he found the opening. But now he was disoriented and continued left, crossed his course before I could stop him and ran down again into the ravine. Try as I might, I could not get him to flank back to the right before turning back. After several futile commands, I retired.

It was only then I realized this trial took your turnback for granted; that was the easy part. The hard part was the number of redirects at the turnback needed to get the dog past the abandoned fencing and on out to the second group of sheep, taking the path up the right side of the field. I had never given Gus redirects after the turnback whistle. I hadn't needed to in US trials if I flanked him correctly before blowing the turnback. This combination completely confused him. He got frantic trying to find his second set and stopped listening to me completely. Yet another surprise course where the difficulties were not obvious to me even though I had watched numerous runs before my turn. When would I see it before I ran it and, more important, anticipate and train it before I ran it?

I was frustrated, but also stimulated by the subtlety of the course requirements. These were issues I had never encountered in the US and had no idea how to train for. I walked up to a group of young men whose runs I had not seen, but who were talking about the course. It was chilly and, with their hats and mufflers on, they were hard to recognize. I did not think I knew any of them. In mock tones, I demanded someone help me with this combination of turnback and repeated redirects. I said we had nothing like this in the US, no abandoned fences anywhere in the west, instead mostly big, uninflected fields, and it was impossible to even practice this. I asked who would agree to help me? As one man, they each pointed to someone else, a witty group. I laughed, then pleaded in earnest. One pointed out kindly that my dog had immediately taken his turnback whistle, so the redirects were the problem, not the turnback. I was grateful for that bit of encouragement and nodded agreement. Just then, an older fellow walked by. They all pointed to him and said loudly that he was the right one to help me.

He turned and stopped, and said, "No, no, I don't do clinics, I don't teach." I said I didn't want a clinic, but rather a private lesson in a place with similar conditions so I could achieve flexible redirects on my dog. We sat down to introduce ourselves and talk more. He was a lovely fellow, kind, grasped the issue immediately, and we discussed it some more. It was only then that I realized that his had been the run that convinced me I understood the course well enough to sign up to run. I talked to him about his run, how I could see him problem-solving as he went along, how intelligently he had run the course. He was gratified. I meant every word. His run was so smooth that I didn't perceive the difficulties until I tried it myself. Later I learned his had been the winning run.

We continued to talk, and he invited me to come out to his farm, on the very northwestern tip of Wales. But he said it could not be very soon because he was in charge of the sheep for the upcoming International in Wales, so it might be two months before we could get together. But he promised we would. I was overjoyed I would get to spend time with this lovely, thoughtful fellow, see another part of Wales, and get another opinion about my dog from someone I respected so much. Though again I failed to understand the course and prepare my dog to negotiate its difficulties, yet I had laid the groundwork for deepening my understanding. I drove home, content that we were another step closer to the heart of our pilgrimage.

Along my travels, I had posted my trial experiences on Facebook. UK trials were so various, the challenges so unexpected, that I was sure my US Facebook friends would find my adventures interesting. I billed Talgarreg as the most difficult course I had ever encountered, described it in detail and made no secret of our failure to complete it. I often referred to Gus on Facebook as Mr. Intrepid, Mr. Natural or Mr. Big Shot. About Talgarreg, I claimed our faults as mine, my failure to work all possible combinations with him to prepare him for the trial. My posts generally attracted much commentary, including some who applauded my "bravery" for even going to the post at such trials.

I realized then that with another dog I might not be so brave, might not be able to admit our faults so readily. With Gus I felt there was no challenge too great to try our mettle on. I knew he would surprise me on the upside, understand the challenge, and work it out on his own, as he had on the long outrun in gale force winds. I loved him so much, had so much faith in him, that stepping to the post with him was a deep privilege. Even if it went bad afterwards, I knew his gather at least would never put us to shame.

The next day back home I went out to my practice field. I closed the gate, turned, and stared. Where there had been twenty-five aging ewes of questionable descent, now there were an additional fifty or so ewes called mules, usually a cross between a Blue Faced Leicester and a Swaledale. They were known for their mottled black and white faces, sturdy build and stolid temperaments. With mules you had to earn every inch. They made a dog work for his living.

I stood looking at them, overjoyed at this opportunity to work fresh sheep. They were lovely, looked to be yearlings. Gus was attentive and worked carefully, taking their measure. They obeyed a dog but needed to be convinced first. I did what I loved doing back home, had Gus shed off a small group of ten to twelve, then had him push them through the gate to the far pasture. The ten moved slowly and tried to deke around to get back to the group. Gus lowered his head and pushed; they would go! The more sheep in the field, the stronger the pressure, the harder he needed to work to keep the two groups apart. I loved these sheep! We were going to have a field day with them! Later the sheep farmer came by to chat. Were the new sheep all right? I praised them emphatically. He said he was afraid I might mind. I assured him I was delighted by them!

*Trainers*

I had thought early and hard about who I would like to have lessons with. So far I had met a lot of handlers, had made some friends, met people in person who were already Facebook friends, and had competed at numerous trials. But I hadn't yet decided who I wanted to work with and, as important, who would work with me. The great luxury of the UK was just how many great handlers there were from whom to choose. In addition to the very top handlers and the most conspicuous ones—those who had already visited the US and given many clinics and lessons, hence signaling they were in the training business—there were many others who also gave lessons and clinics and took dogs in for training, but on a more occasional basis.

There was always the delicate question when talking to one of these experienced handlers of whether one was on the road to becoming a friend or was instead exploiting their expertise without proper compensation. Partly that had to do with how equal one's own level of accomplishment was to theirs. Of course, mine was mostly less, but how much less? So much that it turned me into a supplicant rather than a friend? This concerned me, and I continually looked for clues as to whether I should offer payment for a lesson or whether this would destroy the first buds of a friendship.

It was easy to be misguided about this since I wanted it so much. I had to constantly review our interaction to keep a correct tone and restraint about where I took the conversation. I frequently prepared general topics about the kinds of talent dogs possessed, evolution in training methods, topics I hoped would prove interesting to them and relieve any feelings of exploitation. I felt I might be capable of contributing to these conversations as a quasi-equal and that they might help to establish a bond based on mutual interest, rather than my simply seeking solutions to my own training issues. I remember visiting a young woman, already a very successful handler with her talented youngster. When I told her some of the trainers I had had lessons from, she broke into a cry of excitement and envy that I, as an outsider, could freely ask these champions for a lesson, whereas she, although friends with them, was also a potential competitor, and so could not ask for help. I appreciated the tough spot this put her in!

While mulling all this, I decided to apply to a talented young handler who had been over to the States a few times giving clinics and judging trials. He was in high demand as a trainer, and I assumed he would see me as nothing more than a (much) older woman who had to be spoken to loudly and slowly. I approached him with some trepidation. After several cancellations due to his travel schedule, which began to alarm me as my time in England was limited, he finally made a firm date for lessons. I drove the five hours to his farm, which quickly turned into six and a half as the "Ignore satnav" sign threw me off the route by almost an hour.

His place was hard to find, and I was a half hour late, despite setting out with an hour's cushion. It was in a remote area with barely any street signs, frequent potholes and many unmarked single-track roads. I found the layout of his farm confusing as there seemed to be more than one dwelling and many outbuildings. It lay in open, cleared land and was built of attractive stone as were many houses in that area.

I could see he was displeased about my lateness when I drove up, and I apologized quickly and profusely. We set off for a big open field with sheep widely scattered about, grazing. I feared we had gotten off on the wrong foot, but he listened attentively as I told him of my own and my dogs' weaknesses and what I wanted to work on. As I worked Gus, I could see that he had expected to be critical of him but could not find a great deal to fault. He even complimented me on his high level of obedience. We worked for a while on my handling, on steadying Gus. I liked his thinking. If a steady did not slow my dog sufficiently, he should know that a lie down was coming next. From then on I saw these two commands as an effective sequence I would always follow. This was good discipline; it gave me mental structure. I also told him of Gus's tension, which was palpable. He took that in.

At the end of the lesson I thanked him profusely. It had been very valuable. Despite his initial impatience he was clearly very self-confident, hugely experienced and very smart. No time had been wasted; he was all business. I was supposed to have one lesson before and then one after a local trial which was to be held the following day. His plans had changed; a friend was coming up and he wanted to cancel the lesson the day after. So instead he proposed we go out early the morning of the trial and work the dogs again. I readily agreed and appreciated his accommodating me.

Next morning, we went to another location, where a group of 100 sheep or so were massed along a wide sloping hill. Behind the first hill was a second, where more sheep were grazing. Gus was to gather one half of it, the right side, my youngster Zac, the left. I sent Gus out to the right. He came in behind those on the first hill and started to gather them and fetch them toward us. I blew a turn back whistle which he took promptly, saw a large group behind him, and cast out for them. He was working beautifully, pacing himself, enjoying himself. The whole job was very quiet, peaceful, correct.

Zac, looking serious, was to gather next. After he gathered the first group, I gave him the turnback whistle, which he knew. He flanked first left, then right. I stopped him, gave the whistle again. I waited. He sifted it. Left was wrong, right was wrong. I gave the whistle again; he thought he would try behind him. Went back nicely, over the second hill for the last ones. Good work! The trainer asked if I wanted to send Gus again, said it might be too much for him with a trial to run later in the day. I airily said Gus had plenty of stamina and this was work we could never get again. He said this work should help Gus's tension at the trial later in the day. I sent him one more time and packed up for the trial, very satisfied with my dogs and gratified that the trainer had been so thoughtful about what Gus needed.

After an immense amount of time spent driving up wrong dirt roads, I made a call to the trial host, was set straight, and finally found the trial site. I had some time before my run and had a chance to get to know several people I'd never heard of but liked on the spot. My favorite was the course director, a lovely, bright, articulate, ironic fellow with a gentle, kind sense of humor and a humorous, teasing way about him. I stuck close to him, but not so close that he couldn't do his course directing job, and we talked about some famous dogs, and who among them produced the best pups. I wasn't sure I should ask such indiscreet questions and didn't expect to get an answer, but I did. That impressed me, his musing on this with a perfect stranger. I liked him immediately! I had signed up to run, but didn't know most of the handlers, so no idea when I was up. When he indicated it was my turn, I rushed to grab Gus out of the car, worried about making the judge wait for me. He saw my concern, calmed me and begged me to take my time. How different this was from some US trials, where handlers were instructed to be ready for their run the instant they were up.

We gathered ourselves and walked calmly to the post. The course was of a moderate size, set in a small, grassy, pleasant field enclosed by an ancient stone wall, with one or two shade trees. Sheep called lonks were being run. They were set casually at the top of a slow grade. I realized I had not been watching with any great care, had not considered whether sending right or left was preferable. I was relaxed, and just decided to send Gus right without much thought. I saw him make his way around, giving me his usual lovely outrun, except that near the top he perceptibly slowed. I realized the hill gather in the morning had indeed tired him. He did not stop, though, which would have cost him points.

He pulled up quietly behind his sheep and lifted carefully and slowly. I was prepared to blow a harsh steady but saw I didn't need to. He was bringing them totally correctly on his own with perfect pace and a good line. Quiet around the handler's post, he settled in behind his sheep and drove them in a measured way around the course. His usual tension was nowhere to be seen.

A few corrections to make the panels, and we were in the shed ring. I shed as I always had in the US, having him hold his side while I sidled up on my side, trying to move off the two on the back to open up a hole. The two turned as they went, leaving me a clean hole for a shed, but the turn meant he could not take them on the head. I made a mental note to ask the trainer about that. We went to the pen, our first after my dazzling lesson the day before. Gus brought them slowly. I stepped back, he brought them almost to the mouth. I sidled around behind them, he followed me around to cut off an escape to his side. I stepped into them, then back, asked him *"on your feet!"* to put a bit more pressure on his side, and together we squeezed them in. We were a team, and it went like clockwork. I was elated, heard a couple of whoops and claps.

Later I asked the trainer how I could have improved the shed to enable the two to be taken on the head instead of the tail. He said he would have taken 5 off that shed. The idea was to get the other three sheep to move off, not to move the two I wanted to shed. Some words that the course director had spoken that day came back to me—*"the shed is a dance, isn't it . . ."* —and finally I understood how much indirection there is in good sheep work. If you want to take the two, clear away the three; simply expose the two. I vowed to do it differently from then on.

The judge came out of his box at the end of the day, and I was delighted to learn it was Jim Cropper, the legendary large man, great handler and trainer. He was genial and charming, complimented me on Gus, said he liked him. I later learned that we had come in third, beaten only by two of the most illustrious dogs in the north of England, Ricky Hutchinson's Sweep and Jock. They were to become the Reserve Supreme and Supreme Champion the following year. This was to remain the best placing of our entire stay in the UK.

It was not until many months later that I connected the gathering I had done with the trainer that morning to the perfectly calm work Gus had done at the trial a few hours later. All traces of tension had vanished! I thought back to the trainer's words: *gathering on the hill should help with Gus's tension.* Indeed, it had. I had not seen this relationship before. I now began to ponder the central fact of Gus's mentality: his urgent need to gather. I had described these events to a UK friend, a shepherdess, how the morning gather had calmed Gus, made him totally pliable and exquisite in his work at the trial. She, too, responded that it wasn't that the hill gathering had tired him, it was that *this kind of* work calmed him. Gathering relaxed him, I realized; it satisfied a deep need. Gathering is the basic, instinctual urge that makes a border collie a border collie. All else, the driving, the close work, are added tools that can be taught, but they derive from the natural impulse to gather.

Gus had in fact been telling me this all his life, but I hadn't listened well enough. Gus's mission in life, as he has taken great pains to tell me, is to *bring me sheep.* Once when I questioned an exercise my trainer proposed, she dismissed my fears that it would weaken him. She said, *"You cannot destroy this dog's will to bring you sheep!"* I have always remembered that, and it has helped me take new steps to control his unquenchable urge to fetch them at top speed. When people say, "He's a lot of dog" or "He's a bit full on!" what they see is Gus's inexorable need to bring me sheep. At times I must have imagined that I heard him grunt as he lifted his sheep, the urgency to lift and fetch was so palpable. I had more to learn about the ramifications of this insight, but this was an important step.

In keeping with my desire to experience different trainers' methods, I drove out to visit a top handler in Wales. He lived in one of the most beautiful parts of Wales, the Brecon Beacons, and the countryside was stunning. Sheep were in every pasture, and every pasture was green. It seemed every inch of the countryside was used. There was no shoulder, only hedgerows that did not allow space for a car to pull off the road. I saw breathtaking view after view but could not stop to take pictures. Wales was an easy place to get lost in. Thinking I had followed directions, I ended up at the dead end of a single-track road, parked and waited for 20 minutes without seeing anyone. Of course, I had no phone reception either, so had to turn around and go back out to call. Then, too, I did not yet comprehend that a layby was what we call a turnout, so missed an important landmark. There were no street names, so it was hard even to describe where I was.

Finally, I drove up to a nearby house, knocked and asked whether the householder knew where the trainer lived. I mentioned that he had border collies and sheep, but in Wales that does not narrow the field much. I added that he was a very famous sheepdog handler! Finally, he said he thought I might be looking for the fellow around the corner and left onto the single-track road. I took it and drove up with relief.

I had bought Zac from him two years before, was finding him hard to train and hoped for some advice. My other goal was to show him Gus, to see what he thought of him. He was one of the most successful handlers in the UK, already a Supreme Champion. That summer he would win the International again with a very young bitch. A Facebook friend I liked and trusted told me not to worry that he might be arrogant and standoffish because he was so successful, that he was simply a modest Welsh lad, and I should not be intimidated. This was indeed the person I met. He was friendly, yet formal, helpful and very funny. I explained about Zac that I could not make headway with him. There was something intractable, stubborn, in him that

I could not reach or change. But as much as that, I wanted to show him Gus, to see if he saw what I saw. This visit was an important part of the pilgrimage for me.

After having tea and watching a bit of a soccer match, we went out into his field, boots on. It was always wet in Wales. He had just moved into a new house, a compound with what looked like two houses built together, a metal barn, another old stone barn, and several other outbuildings. One of the houses was being remodeled. There were two fields to work in, connected by a stone wall with openings on both sides.

He wanted to see Zac first. I sent Zac on an outrun for his sheep. As usual, he was ferocious, gobbled up ground, reached his stock in a few fully outstretched strides. He was so light-footed, one was conscious of nothing so much as his dainty white paws flying over the ground. His outrun was ruthless, efficient; it had no cast, he gave the sheep no room. He was behind them in a heartbeat. They were startled and scattered, a few ran back behind him without his noticing. Zac brought the remaining ones with hard directness. I laid him down, but the damage was done. He had roiled these sheep, and they did not trust him.

I turned and said, "We've been working on his outrun for two years"—"and you still don't have it," he broke in. We both laughed uproariously at the frank insult of it. I knew it was kindly meant. I said, "I can't progress with him beyond this point. I go over the same ground every time, and every time he fails to give it to me. I know he understands, though he looks as if he doesn't. I feel as though he's playing me. And another thing: he seems immune to praise. When he shows me some pace and feel on the drive, I reward him, pet him, make much of him, respect him. But does it make his ears go flat back when he looks at me, or produce a genuine smile of pleasure, a sense of oneness with me? No, there is nothing." He promised to take Zac for a few weeks to see whether he could help me with him.

We worked him a few minutes more. Zac continued to work with the same zeal, dispatching his sheep with terrifying directness. Finally, his remaining sheep ran into some dense brush and trees and ended up on the freshly outfitted slate windowsill of the remodeled house, five of them lined up in a row on an eight inch wide sill. It looked as if they were trying to get into the kitchen, to find safety from Zac anywhere they could. The trainer laughed and sent his dog to nudge them back onto the field.

We turned our attention to Gus, who had been watching the sheep while Zac worked. He nodded, and I looked at Gus. Gus was standing now, crouching, eyeing his sheep steadily. I gave him a single soft cluck, the way you might do to barely start a horse. He leaned forward, head down with the border collie crouch and began padding softly toward his sheep, about 200 yards away. The trainer watched him intently. I let Gus walk onto them for fifty yards or so to show his beautiful eye, then mouthed my whistle and gave him the softest possible left flank. Immediately he cast off in his trademark beautiful, pear shaped figure.

His feel for sheep was such that I always felt it almost pained him to flank too close as he cast around his sheep. Leaving the forward motion, he turned his head sideways and cast out, giving exquisite ground, almost equidistant as he circumnavigated his sheep. This was his caress to his sheep. He compensated for the release of pressure by his speed, by the circular curve of his body as he engulfed his sheep and by the power of his eye, which, as soon as he had reached 12 o'clock, locked onto his sheep and held them as he advanced. I blew a second command, a soft high, flat "steady." He slowed by a hair behind his sheep and brought them in a straight line to me. It was always a moment of excitement for me to see him work so beautifully and naturally.

I let him drive for a bit, then we did a quick shed, and he walked two sheep away. We continued to work two sheep while the other three stood and grazed nearby, to demonstrate Gus's power. The two are determined to get back to the others. As they learn to outsmart the dog, they even learn, counterintuitively, to run the opposite way from their companions, drawing the dog off the pressure, then suddenly bolting back. Gus is no longer fooled by this maneuver. He always knows where the draw is to the other sheep and is on guard.

The trainer watched and nodded. He said, "I can see why you don't like Zac. Gus is so natural, he always knows just where to be. You hardly have to say anything to put him in the right spot. Most dogs aren't like that." I told him of Gus's breeding and asked him whether he thought Gus was good enough to breed. "Of course!" he responded, "and with his breeding it would be a shame not to breed him." I felt satisfied. He had helped me with both dogs, helped me feel I was justified in seeking a mate for Gus, and promised to get to the bottom of whether Zac could become a useful dog for me.

While I was in Wales, I ran Gus in the North Wales Sheepdog Championship Trial. It was a beautiful field, a long outrun up the slow grade of a hill. The few other Welsh trials I attended had featured light Welsh sheep, but here the sheep were huge Texel crosses, big as cows, heavy, slow and hard to move. I had never worked this breed before. Texels are not pretty sheep, with their enormous faces, broad, pushed in foreheads and pugnacious expressions. They are stolid and unreactive.

Though the sheep were set very visibly at the top of the field, the white of the sheep contrasting nicely with the green grass, some dogs ran out too wide, went through an opening into the next field, got caught behind a fence, and had to retire. Gus saw them from my feet and ran without incident to the top. Now that he is older, he is more agreeable to a lie down at the top. We had a sideways lift (two off), but a very steady fetch through the middle of the fetch gates (two off), a decent drive and turn through the first drive gate. I had watched the way a very good handler shaped the cross drive and tried to make mine the same. We arrived just a tad below the panels, but then overcorrected and missed the cross-drive gate (nine off).

We had to execute a marked shed, then a single after the pen. These Texel ewes had a different rhythm from mules. They acted as though they would stand their ground and defy the dog, then, at the last minute moved off unpredictably, each one for herself. They were especially heavy on the close work and hard to circulate, but somehow we managed a poor shed.

But the most difficult element was the pen, where I had seen many teams retire after their sheep had run several complete revolutions around the pen, refusing to go in, and the dog was unable to make them. These heavy sheep had beaten the dog. Some simply ran out of time, others retired in futility. In this trial, penning these huge creatures would be the critical test of the dog's power.

I took a deep breath at the pen, opened the gate and asked Gus forward with a single "steady." He began to maneuver them toward the pen and, before I could say anything, deked first left, then right with tight, close flanks. There was some energetic scuffing. He first rushed his sheep, then skidded to a halt without touching them. Dirt was flying. Then he flanked and rushed them on the other side. It looked chaotic. I was shocked, had never seen him do that before. I didn't know what he was doing, and then—*he had them in the mouth of the pen.* I opened my mouth to give him a command, saw they were lined up ready to go in, and shut it again. Still not fully comprehending what he had done, I opened my arms wide automatically, we both inched around to seal the sides, and in they went. We both knew this last maneuver by heart. I don't believe I ever gave him a command after the first steady; the pen took hardly a moment. Zero off. That's Gus knowing his sheep better than I did at a defining moment and taking charge. It was another bit of his magic.

The last element was the marked single. I had to be careful. I didn't want a grip and a DQ after a decent run. We got them back in the shed area, and I found that a marked one was amenable to being separated.

Gus began walking her away, no call from the judge. She swerved, I called to him, "get in," my term for—*get on the pressure, hold it*! He swerved onto the pressure like a magnet attracting metal; the judge called it immediately. Later looking at the scoreboard, I recognized some former or current members of the Welsh team on the roster. We had finished eighth out of 29. Not bad for a field full of top handlers. But for one unfortunate and unnecessary mistake that I made—missing the cross drive—we might have placed in the points. I was happy, praised my champion, left feeling contented.

Our second stay in Cambridge, I had a chance to run the same difficult double gather course in East Anglia that I had run with such dismal results the previous year. We had failed to bring the first set of sheep on the required oblique line across and down through the middle gate. Since then I had practiced this oblique line with Gus diligently *for an entire year*. If I could stop him at 2 o'clock behind his sheep, I could get that line, but if he ran through my stop to 12 o'clock, his tension, his need to bring sheep straight down to me would kick in, and I would be unable to stop him. I felt I knew what I needed to do, and my hopes were correspondingly high.

The day came. As we stood at the post waiting for our first set of sheep to be set, I looked down at Gus. Despite my setting him up on my right side to prepare him to run out to the right, his head was turned sharply left and he was looking intently across my legs to a field far to the left. What, I wondered, is over there? I followed his gaze and saw that the second set of sheep from a prior run was still on the field! They were not supposed to be on the field, but since almost no one had gotten the first set down, the crew decided to leave them out, clearly assuming it wouldn't matter, since no dog would be able to spot them at such a great distance from the post. With Gus's extraordinary eyesight, it mattered to us!

In a strangled voice, I said *"No, this!"* and simultaneously swung my body firmly to the right. He now turned his head as well and scanned the right side of the field. Luckily, at that moment the crew was bringing out his first packet of sheep. He turned and saw, not sheep, but only movement in the low hanging bough of a tree the sheep were set beneath, and locked on, staring fixedly at the correct spot. Later, when I reflected on the events of that afternoon, I was amazed he had spotted the second packet. They must have been 900 yards away on a vast open field and were completely still; not many dogs could have seen them from the post. But what struck me even more acutely was that most dogs would not have agreed so readily to give up a packet of sheep they could clearly see for some partially obscured movement in the brush on the other side of the field, at least not without a lot of convincing. We had never practiced anything like that swiveling sequence at home, but he was very attuned and receptive to my body language. It was a subtle moment and illustrated his keen intelligence and mental flexibility.

I sent him. I believe he must have remembered this course from the previous year, as he ran smoothly across to the fence, out the gate, up into the second field, and across the plank into the third field. As before, the sheep were set at the top of the third field, up a steep grade, and were blind to the dog as he started up the hill. At that point I lost sight of him and could do nothing but wait and look. It was quiet behind me as handlers watched, then I heard someone say in a low voice, "he's behind them."

I looked harder at the sheep. Yes, they had moved closer together and were holding their heads high. I realized he was already at twelve o'clock and quickly tried to flank him back to two o'clock to start the oblique drive to the fetch gates. Superb outrunner that he was, in the third field he had cast out as wide as he could, pressing himself against the fence and into the tall grass that grew up next to it. The best outrunning border collies, when they lose sight of their sheep, instinctively cast out not in, so as not to miss their sheep. But the tall grass camouflaged his progress.

I might have been able to stop him at the right spot, had I been able to see him. I blew another whistle to flank him back to two o'clock, but it was too late. Once at the top, his deeply rooted instinct to *bring me sheep* was so powerful that he could not move off that balance point. How could a dog who had used every bit of instinct to get to that sweet spot be expected to give it up at a single flank whistle? By allowing him to reach twelve o'clock, I had lost everything.

Though for an entire year I had practiced a stop and walk up at two, three and four o'clock along the arc of the outrun, had even practiced reversing him there and sending him around below his sheep, all in order to subdue his strong sense of balance, once he had made the heroic journey to the top, I could not override his instinct. Could the same dog do both? Run out urgently without any help from the handler in that perfect, instinctual way, casting wide and deep until he saw his stock, then apply the finesse and training required to quell that fierce natural urge to fetch sheep by moving back around the circle and driving them sideways? *Mr. Natural, it turned out, was too natural!* But that was what I loved about him. He would die before he would fail to bring me sheep. He had that quality that both shepherds and trialers prized: the unerring ability to find and move his stock by casting exquisitely out wide and deep behind them, leaving them undisturbed, then lifting them from behind and marching them straight toward his shepherd. It could not be fully overridden by training. It was the source of his power. I would not have it any other way. It was very moving to me in a way I cannot explain. It was more important to me than winning.

I thought back to the first time we had run the double lift on this course and had failed to bring the first set of sheep down on the oblique line to the lower field. The compliment I had received from the shepherd reverberated in my ear with new meaning, and I saw now that I had ignored the most important lesson from that failure. On lesser fields, where the outrun was not heroic, but instead rather ordinary, I might be able, with some yelling and insistence, to get Gus to stop at 2 o'clock and lift his sheep at the required 45-degree angle. In other words, if the outrun was not heroic, I could convince Gus to delay gratification, suppress his strong natural balance and the tension that accompanied it, and consent to the oblique fetch. The subtle challenge embedded in the double gather was to juxtapose the most instinctual element in the course—the gather—with the most artful, restrained and refined element—

the oblique fetch. It took a combination of strong natural balance and a refined discipline that could override natural impulses to execute the double gather. Very few dogs had both the power that comes from that instinctual urge and the refinement that denies or delays that urge.

The preference for either the natural dog with strong balance or the refined dog with precision and pace is a recurring theme in the rivalry that has long existed between UK shepherds on one hand and farmers and hobbyists on the other. Some shepherds scorn trial dogs as weak and not up to handling the emergencies that occur daily on the moors and fells. Shepherds need a dog who can run wide, gather large flocks off the hill, and leave no sheep behind. Trialers, on the other hand, want a dog that can win the trial by steadying his sheep, making panels, and exhibiting sensitive footwork, pace, and style. But the effect on dogs undergoing an intensive training regime at an early age in order to trial successfully can be that such a regime weakens their instinctual impulses, such as balance, and lessens their power. *Every whistle feels like a correction to a dog.* Trialers, on the other hand, sometimes regard shepherd's dogs as "blokes" lacking refinement, pace, and rigorous training. But some dogs that have been trained to a high standard at an early age are sold when they are older because they cannot complete a course with difficult sheep. Their training has weakened their ability to do the basic job.

Once at a training session in England, Gus lost patience and gripped his sheep. The trainer criticized him for being "low class." I protested, "he's a dog! He knows nothing of class." That a dog would be described in such socially motivated terms gave me an insight into the notion that pace, style, and subtlety are identified with "classy" dogs, not "blokes," and that notions of class have filtered down into training methods and breeding preferences in the sheepdog world. The balance between instinct and training is a delicate one, is different for each dog, and must be protected. It is a thorny issue and is an art in the hands of the best trainers.

The balance between the bloke and the classy dog might have been in the judge's mind that day. As we were walking off, he came out of his booth and said, "Don't be too angry with him. That's a very decent dog you've got there." High praise, indeed, despite our failure.

# Chapter 3: A Reckoning

Now that I had shown Gus to a number of top handlers, I was starting to feel justified in breeding him. I had had several gratifying experiences in the UK that proved his worth. Once, at a trial in Northumberland, even though we did not do particularly well, the judge sprinted over to me at the end and asked if he could breed a bitch to Gus. I didn't know him, though later learned he'd been on his national team numerous times and was a respected trialer and trainer. His interest puzzled me because we had hardly begun our run when one of Gus's sheep took off and we had to retire. He said, "Ah know, but there was just soomptin' about him that ah liked." I offered to visit him and give him a better look at Gus, which I did, and we became friends.

I had first begun to think about breeding Gus in the US the year before we first went to England. It was then that I noticed that others with good males aggressively courted owners of worthy bitches. We had not done this but also had not been approached. When I finally forced myself to campaign him with bitch owners, I got various answers, "Yes, Gus is on my short list" or "Oh, I never thought of Gus" to "Hmm, he's quite a lot of dog for me" or "I think I need something quieter for this bitch."

There were a few people with nice bitches who did want to breed to Gus, but one of them only came to feel this after she saw him work at home, rather than at a trial. Then she saw his absolute dedication, how quietly he could work, his feel, precision, flexibility of mind and immense care for his sheep. At home he worked with far less tension but retained his total concentration and sense of responsibility. Many wonderful qualities of a talented dog are evident in daily work that rarely come out at a trial or are not noticed. Here are a few more highlights from Gus's work on and off the trial field:

- A friend was working some of my unruly sheep in my practice field when they suddenly took off over a hill, attracted by a large herd of cattle massed on the other side. My friend called her dog and walked off as the sheep ran away. She didn't want him hurt by a steer! This was the field I worked in, my responsibility. I had no choice but to send Gus, though by now the four sheep were over the hill and out of sight and who knows how deeply embedded among the cattle. The hill blocked my view, so I had to send him blind. I waited, scarcely breathing. Two outcomes occurred to me: Gus would come back empty-handed, and we would have to trek after the runaways, or Gus would fetch the entire Black Angus herd over the hill, fifty huge cows galloping hazardously toward me in an open field. Nothing for many anxious seconds, then I saw ears pierce the horizon. Seconds later, the four ewes appeared over the hill so tightly gathered, Gus so firmly in charge, that their knees knocked against each other.

- Gus could communicate expertly. He would shoot me a look, and it was always clear what he meant. Once a ewe in a packet was limping; I wanted to let her drift away from the group and not be worked. He slowed behind her, then looked at me. "No" was not the right command, because it implied he was being reprimanded. Several seconds passed before I could find the words, "Leave it."

- Once when he was still quite young, before I grasped how quickly he understood things, I spent some time berating him for something. Finally he gave me a look that clearly said, "I get it, now let's move on, there's work to be done! Boss, are you pouting?" I told that story to my trainer. Some years later, while she was training him for a couple of weeks, she got the same look!

- I was preparing Gus for a hill trial. I wanted him to stay on the ridge as he ran out, rather than disappear over the hill where I could not see him. I practiced this on a much smaller hill on my field and whistled him back onto the ridge each time he started to go out of sight. After he showed he understood this, we went back to the truck to rest. Just then our sheep sprinted away and ran over the hill and out of sight. I sent him after them. When he got to the ridge, he stopped, looked at me and said, "Boss, you told me not to go over the ridge." I answered, "Yes, I know what I said, but now you have to get the sheep; they've gone over the hill." Without another word he turned and shot over the hill.

- I was at a trial where the sheep were exceptionally touchy and became unsettled in the shed ring when dog and handler tried to make a hole for the dog to come through. I decided to lie Gus down across from me and settle the sheep myself. I could see he thought that was a mistake, but he obeyed. I sidled slowly toward the sheep, still bunched. Without warning, the leader took off for the exhaust pen, followed by a second ewe, their pace quickening. Without leaving his lie down position, Gus snapped his head around in a sort of flank motion; *he flanked with his head!* His power was such that he stopped the ewes with a turn of his head! The lead sheep took one more step, then stopped; the second ewe stopped behind her. This left a perfect hole between the two groups. I called Gus in briskly and we easily shed our last two sheep "on the head." He had controlled his sheep with a single movement of his head! I had never heard of this until I later read an account of Julie Hill's Supreme Champion Moss, who could hold sheep back with just a turn of his head.

Gus is an "exceptional" dog—my trainer's words, not mine, though she adds, hard to run and not for everybody. That is no doubt the reason he has had few breeding opportunities despite his exceptional talent. He typically placed, but rarely won trials in his later years. And his exceptional qualities are hard to describe and not visible to everyone. In fact, I don't even know what an exceptional dog is, except for the one I have. I don't know what innovations other dogs are capable of, what magic they possess. I only know the magic mine has shown me. There are, beyond a doubt, many exceptional working border collies, each with his own special qualities.

In the UK, I hoped to draw handlers out on this subject. Some recounted stories of similarly uncanny feats during gathering or lambing that I simply listened to in amazement, transfixed and unable to grab pen and paper fast enough to write them down. But stories of feats on the trial field were rare; I put it down to the considerable modesty and humility I saw among UK trialers that prevented them from telling these stories. There is no catalogue of such qualities; the universe of innovations the working border collie can execute is not defined. Are the exceptional ones, by definition, the dogs the best handlers win with? Or are there many exceptional dogs, like Gus, yoked to a handler of vastly less ability, like myself?

I bought my most recent youngster, Ted, on the strength of a Welsh shepherd telling me with wonder in his voice what his brother's dog could do. That dog had the same sire as Ted. I could tell by the way his voice dropped and slowed that this dog continued to surprise with his uncanny understanding and talent. His brother had placed third in the International with this dog. I reasoned that if he was that good, instead of buying a pup off *him*, I would buy a dog off his sire, a respected stud, and hope to get a dog similar to his. I did, and happily have a youngster with an excellent mind, strong concentration, and calmness of spirit. He is just two but is precocious and has been running in the Open class already for several months. Will he inspire in me the same (or different) wonder that Gus does? I don't know yet, but this step toward the next generation had to be taken, and I calculated my best chance was to get a breeding that inspired wonder in someone else.

I bought him from a talented Swedish handler living in Scotland. I went to visit him, interested in a different dog, but he kindly brought out all his and his wife's dogs and demonstrated them. It was quite a show and soon had my head spinning. I felt overwhelmed in the same way I had felt at the Skipton auction. I saw the dog I had come to buy and wasn't sure about him. But then he brought out another youngster, not yet two. As he walked through the gate into the training field with Ted by his side, Ted raised his head to the man walking beside him and threw him a look that said, "What do you need, Boss? I'm ready." That look, more than anything I saw him do that afternoon, drew me to him. It bespoke both a kind of vulnerability and a strong spirit of teamwork.

That evening I took a deep breath and made an offer on him. Then I first learned that he was not meaning to sell Ted, but only to show him. This handler had only had him for a few months, but, he said, Ted was coming along like "gangbusters." In his Swedish accent, this slang word became "gangboosters." I always remembered that because, even in my novice training hands, he continued to come on like gangbusters. Nothing else described his progress so well. You taught it to him on Monday, he had it on Tuesday and continued to show it to you on Wednesday. I had never seen a dog progress so quickly. He was the kind of dog that made you feel you must be a good trainer. The defining and remarkable quality about Ted was his spirit of partnership. One did not have to fight him or his instincts. In this, he was the "un-Gus." The look he threw his handler, and that I intercepted, told the whole story. Over time, I became more and more grateful that his owner and I had agreed on terms and that he had sold me a dog of such honesty, integrity and intelligence.

Will he have the dazzling talent of Gus? A well-known breeder who judged a trial I ran at in England came over to me after Gus gripped and was disqualified. He said, "I had to DQ you, but you can hardly take your eyes off him, he's so exciting." I know what he meant: the electric eye that holds sheep to him, the fineness of the footwork, the stylish stalky stance and perfectly held tail, the urgency with which he commands his stock, the focus and the electric connection between him and his stock. I don't yet know whether Ted will make me feel the way Gus has. I respect Ted enormously, and I expect to win more trials with him than with Gus. He is more obedient, and I do not have to fight his instinct. But will I step to the post in the knowledge that my canine partner will always have a beautiful, urgent outrun, will always find his sheep and will always bring them to my feet, and that, in doing so, he is fulfilling an age old instinct that is the basis of the breed's natural ability to work stock? That urge is both Gus's greatest talent and his greatest flaw.

# *Epilogue*

It came to me when I was doodling around on Facebook: *you accept the flaws you can live with to get the talents you can't live without*. It seems so simple, yet I have struggled for the right perspective almost the entire life of this dog, who has meant so much to me, but whose flaws have repeatedly tested my loyalty. For yes, we must be loyal to our dogs, not parade their faults before the world, nor treat them with the same careless disregard we apply to ourselves. Unlike us, they give their all, every day, and risk a lot in doing so. Why has it taken me the span of this dog's life to formulate that sentence? Why did I doubt him for so long in the face of his massive talent, and diminish his achievements by my own inadequate handling? If I'm honest, I must admit my part in failing to temper his flaws, reduce them to manageable proportions, let the talent shine through.

In my defense, I will say that Gus was a dog without tension when young and that, contrary to the usual progression, his tension grew with age. It began when he was about 6, and it took me the better part of a year to name and acknowledge the change in him and to seek the help I needed to deal with it. It was not until I met a respected trainer who had owned his uncle (and had won the US national nursery championship with him) that I gained some insight into how to recognize his tension and, to some extent, how to control it. It did not help that during his fifth year, he got a painful groin pull, which put him out of commission, between the healing and the physical therapy, for the better part of a year. When he was sound again, he was a somewhat different dog.

It's not that I didn't try. I campaigned him, sought one expert after another, both in the US and the UK, learned invaluable things from each. But it has been a mosaic: no one expert has had the entire answer. I painstakingly fitted pieces together over time and finally have been able to tell his story, make sense of it, give him his full due while acknowledging his faults.

What I finally understood was Gus's deep instinctual urge to bring me sheep and the strong sense of balance that went with it. It was strong, and it would not be denied. One friend characterized our run at the East Anglian double lift as "heroic," and that was the right word for it. But what I had not yet grasped was the subtlety of the double lift and the reason for our repeated failure to execute it. The dog must do a heroic first outrun. Then, right after that, he is not allowed to bring them straight down to you—No! He must tolerate the indirection of bringing them on an oblique line to a cone still 100 yards in front of you. For Gus, fetching on that oblique line deeply frustrated his natural impulses. It made sense to me that the most difficult course, the double gather, would cunningly juxtapose the greatest instinctual feat—that of doing a heroic 800 or so yard outrun—with the highest level of training and control—bringing the sheep on an oblique fetch line. Right in those first two elements, the double gather combined the talents of the most natural outrunner with the learned skills and restraint of the most schooled dog. He had to be exceptional at both ends of this spectrum to win the day.

Handlers readily agree—all dogs have their faults. I've heard that all my years in the border collie world, paid lip service to it, but did not know the hard, deep truth of it, did not understand what instincts drove both the talents and the faults, did not see the broad connection between disparate behaviors. My US trainer first opened my eyes with one such axiom, "Over-flanking is associated with not listening." A top UK trainer said apropos of nothing at all, after Gus and I had trained with him for three intensive days together, and it came from a depth within him I had not seen before, "I think you need to run him with occasional lie-downs on the fetch. Don't try to manage it with just a steady." Now I understand what a concession that was to Gus's "full on" forward motion and his tension, since in the UK the goal is to run a dog who paces consistently and naturally and does not break it up with unsightly lie downs. This trainer had obviously been sifting it within himself and spoke only the conclusion aloud. He had seen how hard it was to curb Gus's tension and concluded a constant steady pace was an impossible strategy for him.

The "talent you can't live without" is the magic in this story. The fine beauty of it, the rightness of the dog's work to the type of sheep you are shepherding that day, the created unity between dog and handler, their joint understanding of the task at hand and how to perform it, is the continuing marvel. When fine working collies get old and die, their handlers announce it on Facebook along with their final permission and blessing, which I will say to my dog when the moment comes, "Run free, Gus." In that canine afterlife, footfalls can do no wrong, and instinct and craft are finally and fully united. My UK friend, the judge who admired Gus, put it well. "He runs from the heart," he said. "The best ones do." I cannot say fairer than that.

Lightning Source UK Ltd.
Milton Keynes UK
UKHW022150211220
375642UK00009B/209